Slavery, War, and a New Birth of Freedom

1840s–1877

Editorial Advisers

HISTORY THROUGH LITERATURE
AMERICAN VOICES, AMERICAN THEMES

Slavery, War, and a New Birth of Freedom

1840s–1877

Jeffrey H. Hacker, Editor

LONDON AND NEW YORK

First published 2014 by M.E. Sharpe

Published 2015 by Routledge
2 Park Square, Milton Park, Abingdon, Oxon OX14 4RN
711 Third Avenue, New York, NY, 10017, USA

Routledge is an imprint of the Taylor & Francis Group, an informa business

Cover images (clockwise from top left) provided by: AP Photo; Reza Estakhrian/Getty Images; Kean Collection/Getty Images.

Interior images provided by: Kean Collection/Getty Images, p. 5; Hulton Archive/Getty Images, p. 14; Hulton Archive/Getty Images, p. 22; AP Photo/Amherst College Archives and Special Collections, and the Emily Dickinson Museum, p. 39; AP Photo, p. 46; The Granger Collection, NYC—All rights reserved, p. 57; Hulton Archive/Getty Images, p. 74; Interim Archives/Getty Images, p. 95; Reza Estakhrian/Getty Images, p. 129; The Granger Collection, NYC—All rights reserved, p. 143; Hulton Archive/Getty Images, p. 154; Time Life Pictures/Mansell/Time Life Pictures/Getty Images, p. 163; Library of Congress, p. 178; Library of Congress, p. 186.

The EuroSlavic fonts used to create this work are © 1986–2013 Payne Loving Trust.
EuroSlavic is available from Linguist's Software, Inc.,
www.linguistsoftware.com, P.O. Box 580, Edmonds, WA 98020-0580 USA
tel (425) 775-1130.

Library of Congress Cataloging-in-Publication Data

Slavery, war, and a new birth of freedom, 1840s–1877 / Jeffrey H. Hacker, Editor.
pages cm. — (History through literature : American voices, American themes)
(Sharpe insights)
Includes bibliographical references and index.
ISBN 978-0-7656-8341-0 (cloth : alk. paper) — ISBN 978-0-7656-8324-3 (pbk. : alk. paper)
ISBN 978-0-7656-8325-0 (electronic)
1. United States—History—1849–1877—Sources. 2. United States—Intellectual life—19th century—Sources. 3. American literature—19th century. 4. Slavery in literature. 5. United States—History—Civil War, 1861–1865—Literature and the war. 6. Literature and history—United States—19th century. I. Hacker, Jeffrey H., editor of compilation.

E415.7.S63 2014
973.6—dc23 2013010946

ISBN 13: 9780765683410 (hbk)
ISBN 13: 9780765683243 (pbk)

Contents

Preface

History Through Literature: Slavery, War, and a New Birth of Freedom (1840s–1877) is the third in a six-volume series designed to support interdisciplinary coursework and independent reading in American history and letters. The material presented in each volume is selected and organized to enrich the study of the nation's historical record, its literary heritage, and their mutual influences.

Each volume begins with a chronology that identifies, defines, and places in context the key historical events, literary works, authors' lives, and cultural movements of the period in question. The centerpiece of the volume is a comprehensive overview essay that highlights the era's major historical trends, social and cultural movements, literary voices, and landmark works as reflections of each other and the spirit of the times. The core content comprises some 20–30 shorter articles—all drawn from the archives of the Sharpe Reference and Sharpe Online Reference imprints—on lives and works in period literature, including extended excerpts. Special features called *Sidelights* apply a different lens to this exploration, focusing on historical literature as a commentary on both the time of the events and the time of the writing. In the present volume, for example, *Sidelights* consider the Civil War in historical fiction and the rediscovery of early African American literature in recent decades.

Throughout the series, the designation of historical and literary "periods" is not bound by strict start–end dates or specific events (with such notable exceptions as national independence, the Civil War, the Great Depression, and World War II). The lives and works of writers obviously overlap any arbitrarily defined eras, and their styles and themes often evolve in ways that defy neat historical classification. Thus, the designation of historical periods and the selection of subjects in each volume are guided by subjective judgments based on a confluence of factors—historical events, social and economic trends, and the rise and decline of artistic and cultural movements.

This volume in particular is defined less by chronological boundaries than by the issues and themes at the heart of national affairs in the mid-nineteenth century. Whereas "America's original sin" of slavery and the movement to oppose it were touched on briefly in the previous volume (*The Early Republic and Rise of National Identity: 1783–1861*), they form the core content—along with the trauma of the Civil War and its aftermath—of the present text.

The title of this volume alludes to one of the great political and oratorical landmarks of the period, rising to the level of literature in the highest sense. The phrase "new birth of freedom" comes from the last line of Abraham Lincoln's iconic speech of 1863, the Gettysburg Address (discussed and reproduced in full in a dedicated chapter):

> *. . . we here highly resolve that these dead shall not have died in vain, that this nation, under God, shall have a new birth of freedom, and that government of the people, by the people, for the people, shall not perish from the earth.*

The articles and excerpts collected in this work thus represent a literary testament to slavery and the individuals who experienced it; the moral campaign to restrict, contain, and finally abolish it; the fratricidal four-year war between the federal Union and the secessionist Confederacy; and the 12-year postbellum era of reconciliation and reconstruction. Writings include personal narratives by slaves and freedmen, a battlefield nurse, a Union general, and the wife of a Confederate officer; novels, short stories, poems, speeches, and a hymn; works that were popular and influential at the time and works that were little known or not even published until decades later. Not overlooked are notable authors and enduring works of the period that were far removed from the brutality of slavery and war, from Emily Dickinson and her delicate, hushed verse to John Muir and Bret Harte and their depictions of the mountains, mining camps, and open skies of the American West.

Carefully read and fully appreciated, great works of literature stand as reliable documents of political, social, intellectual, and cultural history no less than as artifacts of individual creative inspiration.

They provide a record of the past more alive and more vital than any textbook, timeline, or chronicle of public events ever could offer. Thus, the authors and writings presented in this volume—prose and poetry, fiction and nonfiction—offer students, teachers, and casual readers compelling examples in the study of both history though literature and literature through history.

Chronology

1820 In an effort to settle the sectarian dispute over slavery, Congress passes the Missouri Compromise. The agreement admits Missouri to the Union as a slave state, adds Maine as a free state, and establishes 36°30′ north latitude as the dividing line between free and slave states. The compromise will help keep the peace for three decades.

1831 Radical abolitionist William Lloyd Garrison publishes the first issue of his antislavery newspaper *The Liberator.* Garrison becomes the foremost spokesman of the antislavery movement, his newspaper its leading platform.

Nat Turner launches the bloodiest slave rebellion in U.S. history. The insurrection is put down, and Turner is hanged. While awaiting trial, he dictates his account of the events to lawyer Thomas Ruffin Gray, who publishes the narrative as *The Confessions of Nat Turner.*

1838–39 U.S. troops forcibly remove more than 15,000 Choctaw Indians from Georgia to present-day Oklahoma. Thousands die along the way in what comes to be called the Trail of Tears.

1845 Frederick Douglass publishes his *Narrative of the Life of Frederick Douglass, an American Slave,* which wins countless volunteers to the abolitionist cause.

1846 Abolitionist and pacifist Henry David Thoreau refuses to pay delinquent poll taxes as a protest against slavery and the Mexican-American War, and spends a night in jail. The event inspires his 1849 essay "Resistance to Civil Government," or "Civil Disobedience."

1848 The discovery of gold in California attracts hundreds of thousands of fortune seekers from across the United States and other countries, accelerating Western settlement.

Advocates for women's rights attend the movement's first organized gathering in the United States, held in Seneca Falls, New York.

1849 Henry Brown, a 44-year-old plantation slave from outside Richmond, Virginia, escapes bondage inside a crate shipped from Richmond to Philadelphia. Brown recounts the adventure in a book titled *Narrative of the Life of Henry Box Brown.*

1850–60 Traffic on the Underground Railroad, a clandestine network to transport runaway slaves to freedom in the Northern states and Canada, reaches its peak.

1850 Under the Compromise of 1850, the fate of slavery in territories entering the Union will be determined by "popular sovereignty" (voters decide); the agreement also includes a stronger Fugitive Slave Law. Intended to resolve the sectional dispute over slavery, the legislative package merely postpones escalation of the conflict.

1851 Herman Melville's *Moby-Dick,* the story of an obsessed sea captain bent on revenge against a great white whale, is published to mixed reviews. Twentieth-century literary critics will view the whaling ship *Pequod* as a symbol of the "ship of state," its crew as a microcosm of American society, and its calamitous fate as a premonition of civil war.

1852 Harriet Beecher Stowe publishes *Uncle Tom's Cabin; or, Life Among the Lowly,* a searing critique of slavery and the best-selling literary work of nineteenth-century America.

1854 The Kansas-Nebraska Act formally repeals the Missouri Compromise and extends popular sovereignty to all new U.S. territories.

1855 Walt Whitman publishes the first edition of his free-verse collection *Leaves of Grass*. The volume, expanded in eight subsequent editions, will be celebrated as a literary masterpiece and a landmark in the development of a national idiom.

1859 In an attempt to incite a national slave revolt, a group of abolitionists led by John Brown raids a federal arsenal in the Virginia town of Harpers Ferry. Brown is captured and hanged, but the incident pushes sectarian tensions over slavery to the breaking point.

Harriet Wilson's *Our Nig: Sketches from the Life of a Free Black* becomes the first novel by an African American author to be published in the United States. The work will be lost for more than a century and rediscovered in the early 1980s.

1860 The slave population of the United States approaches 4 million.

Republican Abraham Lincoln is elected president on a promise to halt the spread of slavery. South Carolina secedes from the Union, followed by six more Southern states.

Emily Dickinson, withdrawing into seclusion, begins the most productive period of her life as a poet. Within the next five years, she will write many of her nearly 1,800 poems.

1861 On April 12, Confederate cannons open fire on Fort Sumter, a federal stronghold in the harbor of Charleston, South Carolina. The shots mark the onset of the Civil War.

Former slave Harriet Jacobs publishes a narrative of her brutal life in bondage and her escape via the Underground Railroad, titled *Incidents in the Life of a Slave Girl*.

1862 With war raging between North and South, the lyrics to Julia Ward Howe's patriotic "Battle Hymn of the Republic" appear on the cover of *The Atlantic Monthly* in February.

1863 President Lincoln issues the Emancipation Proclamation on January 1, declaring free all slaves residing in states in rebellion against the federal government. The executive order makes clear that the war is being fought to end slavery as well as to restore the Union.

President Lincoln delivers the Gettysburg Address to dedicate the Soldiers' National Cemetery in Gettysburg, Pennsylvania, on November 19.

1865 On April 9, Confederate general Robert E. Lee surrenders his Army of Northern Virginia to Union commander Ulysses S. Grant at Appomattox Court House, Virginia, bringing an end to the Civil War.

On April 14, President Lincoln is shot by Southern sympathizer John Wilkes Booth while attending the popular stage comedy *Our American Cousin* in Washington, D.C. The president will die early the next morning.

The Thirteenth Amendment to the U.S. Constitution, abolishing slavery throughout the United States, is ratified on December 6.

1865–68 Southern states pass restrictive legislation, referred to as "Black Codes," that seeks to nullify the federal rights granted to former slaves and to restore the old slave society.

1867 Radical Republicans seize control of Reconstruction from President Andrew Johnson and break up the South into five military districts occupied by the Union army.

1868 The Fourteenth Amendment extends full U.S. citizenship to all African Americans.

1868–69 Louisa May Alcott's classic children's novel *Little Women,* based on the author's experiences growing up with three sisters, is published in two volumes.

Bret Harte gains national attention with two short stories of pioneer life in mid-century California, "The Luck of Roaring Camp" followed by "The Outcasts of Poker Flat."

1869 The Transcontinental Railroad reaches completion at Promontory Summit, Utah.

1869–77 Beginning in Tennessee, Southern whites gradually reassert control of state governments, and conservative Democrats supplant Northern carpetbaggers and African Americans in dominating governorships and legislatures.

1870 The Fifteenth Amendment grants the vote to African American males. The promise of full enfranchisement will not be realized for nearly a century, however, as Southern states institute poll taxes, literacy tests, and other measures to stifle the black vote.

Senator Hiram Rhodes Revels of Mississippi and Representative Joseph Rainey of South Carolina become the first African Americans to serve in the U.S. Congress.

1872 African American poet, novelist, and social reformer Frances Ellen Watkins Harper produces *Sketches of Southern Life,* a collection of poems and one short story that dramatize the experience of Reconstruction through the eyes of a former slave.

1876 Mark Twain publishes his first novel, *The Adventures of Tom Sawyer,* inspired by his boyhood in a small river town on the Mississippi River.

1877 After the disputed 1876 presidential election and a compromise between the Republican and Democratic parties, the last remaining federal troops are withdrawn from the South. Reconstruction comes to an end.

The Literature of Slavery, Civil War, and Reconstruction

Creative writing in the United States during the antebellum, Civil War, and Reconstruction eras examined the hopes, regrets, and dilemmas of people from every region and every background regarding the defining issues and events of the times. Preeminent among these were the institution of slavery, the movement to abolish it, the war of secession over it, the restoration of national unity, and the experience of former slaves in adjusting to life as free citizens.

Given the profound effects of these issues on the lives of so many Americans, the passions they aroused, and the deeply held principles on which they turned, it is perhaps not surprising that the most influential writings of this period took a greater variety in form and format—and had a greater impact on popular opinion and the course of events—than those in less tumultuous times. The literary legacy of slavery, abolitionism, the Civil War, and Reconstruction takes the form of verse and song; novels and short stories; memoirs, journals, and full-length autobiographies; speeches and editorials; and works in a whole new genre, the slave narrative. The heritage of the period includes writings by men and women in bondage and high office, the North and the South, the infantry and the home front, the cotton field, the plantation house, and the shadows of the Underground Railroad.

Few works in the annals of American literature have had a greater an impact on popular values and the course of events than Harriet Beecher Stowe's antislavery novel *Uncle Tom's Cabin* (1852), the *Narrative of the Life of Frederick Douglass, an American Slave* (1845), William Lloyd Garrison's abolitionist editorials in *The Liberator* (1831–1865), or Abraham Lincoln's second inaugural address in 1865. And what words, written in times of crisis, have remained more familiar to Americans to the present day than those of the Gettysburg Address and the "Battle Hymn of the Republic"?

Not to be overlooked in the great literature of these decades are writings far removed from, and unrelated to, the issues of human bondage and sectional conflict—works emanating from the open spaces of the West (such as Bret Harte's stories of the California Gold Rush, Mark Twain's comic sketches of pioneer life, and John Muir's descriptions of the Sierra Nevada); from the quiet corners of New England (such as Louisa May Alcott's *Little Women,* Henry David Thoreau's *Walden,* and the poetry of Emily Dickinson); and from other far-flung settings and perspectives (such as Nathaniel Hawthorne's novels of Puritan American and Walt Whitman's poems of working-class America and the universal spirit).

Slave Narratives

Firsthand accounts of the misery and degradation of slave life captured the attention of the American reading public as early as the late eighteenth century and fueled a sense of moral outrage that would find expression in the organized abolitionist movement, the Underground Railroad, and efforts by politicians to block the spread of the "peculiar institution" and finally end it. The first of such works was the highly popular *Interesting Narrative of the Life of Olaudah Equiano* (1789), which recounted the capture of an African boy from the Ibo tribe, his transport to America as a slave, and his eventual life as a freedman and antislavery advocate. The single most influential of the slave memoirs was Frederick Douglass's *Narrative of the Life of Frederick Douglass, an American Slave* (1845), whose dramatic account and sheer moral power attracted untold numbers of converts to the abolitionist cause; the book went into nine printings in three years. Rivaling Douglass's book in popularity and sales was William Wells Brown's less rhetorical, less heroic *Narrative of William W. Brown, A Fugitive Slave* (1847), which in revised and expanded form also gained a large readership in Europe.

Notable works penned by former slave women include Harriet Jacobs's *Incidents in the Life of a Slave Girl* (1861), published under the pseudonym Linda Brent and not widely read until the late twentieth century, which relates the brutality to which she was subjected as a child and young adult, her seven years in hiding, and her escape via the Underground Railroad; and Frances Ellen Watkins Harper's Reconstruction-era *Sketches of Southern Life* (1872), which dramatizes the struggles, faith, and perseverance of the proud ex-slave and Harper surrogate Aunt Chloe.

As in Jacobs's memoir, the Underground Railroad figures prominently in the narratives of a number of former slaves. Unsurpassed for pure drama and adventure is the *Narrative of the Life of Henry Box Brown* (1849), about a Virginia plantation slave who escapes in a dry goods crate shipped to Philadelphia by a Richmond storekeeper; after 26 hours inside, Brown emerges a free man. Even more moving is the *Narrative of the Life and Adventures of Henry Bibb, an American Slave* (1849), in which the author describes his initial escape to Canada and his repeated returns to Kentucky to rescue his wife and child—never successfully. William Still, a free black from Philadelphia who served as an organizer and conductor in the clandestine network, compiled the most complete firsthand account of operations, *The Underground Railroad* (1872), including the story of every one of the 649 slaves he helped escape.

A different kind of slave memoir, published in a climate of fear and anger across the South, recounts the largest and bloodiest slave rebellion of the antebellum era. In *The Confessions of Nat Turner* (1832), the leader of more than 60 Virginia slaves who rose up against their owners declares that he was destined by God to deliver his people from bondage and that he received a "sign in the heavens" when the revolt was to begin. Before white militia quelled the uprising, at least 150 individuals lay dead. Turner, who was hanged on November 11, 1831, dictated his historic account to lawyer Thomas Ruffin Gray while in prison. By the time *The Confessions* appeared in print the following year, state legislatures across the South had passed laws that restricted even free blacks from owning weapons or preaching in public and that forbade whites from teaching blacks to read.

Patriotism and the Union Cause

The cause of abolition, the looming prospect of Southern secession, and the actuality of civil war generated a flood of antislavery and patriotic Union writing—much of it of the highest order—in verse and prose. Beginning in January 1831 and for the next 35 years, Boston editor William Lloyd Garrison established himself as the leading voice of radical abolitionism as publisher of the antislavery weekly *The Liberator.* The paper became the official organ of the New England Anti-Slavery Society, and Garrison's impassioned editorials remained a source of inspiration to the entire movement through December 1865.

Uncle Tom's Cabin *gave millions of Americans their first view of human bondage through the eyes of slaves.*

In strictly literary circles, popular early antislavery writings included the first series of James Russell Lowell's *Biglow Papers* (1848), a folksy but scathing satire on slavery and the Mexican-American War in the vernacular of a fictional New England farmer named Hosea Biglow. In the second series (1867), Lowell—through Biglow—muses on patriotism, the pathos and valor of the war, Confederate president Jefferson Davis, the Emancipation Proclamation, and, finally, the ignominies of Reconstruction. Satire aside, the series gave thanks for "a nation saved, a race delivered." Quaker John Greenleaf Whittier, with Lowell a member of the so-called Fireside Poets, published a succession of virulently antislavery poems in the 1840s and 1850s, including "Ichabod" in response to Senator Daniel Webster's defection from the abolitionist cause to support the Compromise of 1850 and the Fugitive Slave Act. Two years later, Harriet Beecher Stowe's *Uncle Tom's Cabin* gave millions of Americans their first view of human bondage through the eyes of slaves themselves. The novel sold 300,000 copies in 1852 alone, with subsequent printings and a stage adaptation putting it before millions of pairs of eyes in the years that followed. The outrage and pathos it generated helped elevate the cause of abolition to a popular movement and move the nation closer to war.

The outbreak of fighting in April 1861 pumped a new level of patriotism into Northern writings—or at least the works that have gone down as the era's classics. Julia Ward Howe's now-familiar lyrics to the "Battle Hymn of the Republic," published in *The Atlantic Monthly* in February 1862, inspired Union soldiers marching into combat and, over time, became a patriotic anthem for the entire nation. On November 19 of the following year, President Abraham Lincoln dedicated a new soldiers' cemetery near the battlefields of Gettysburg, Pennsylvania, with 272 words that became the most cherished statement of national principle

Few works of literature have had a more direct effect on the course of history than Harriet Beecher Stowe's antislavery novel *Uncle Tom's Cabin*, which pushed the nation toward civil war.

and patriotic resolve in the annals of American oratory—the Gettysburg Address.

More popular at the time, however, was an allegorical tale by Edward Everett Hale that appeared in the December issue of *The Atlantic Monthly* titled "The Man Without a Country." The story was inspired by the real-life case of former U.S. congressman and pacifist Clement Vallandigham of Ohio, who was banished behind Confederate lines for denouncing the military draft and inciting resistance to the Union war effort; Vallandigham later renounced his U.S. citizenship and moved to Canada. The protagonist in "The Man Without a Country," likewise banished for an act of treason, in the end is overwhelmed by nostalgia for "my own, my native land." In the darkest months of the Civil War, Hale's cautionary tale was extolled as a statement of patriotic allegiance.

No participant in the Civil War produced a more comprehensive and concise record of the events than the Union general and eventual president Ulysses Grant in his Personal Memoirs (1885). Written as he was dying, to raise money for his family, and published by Mark Twain, the two-volume memoir is widely acclaimed as one of the great autobiographies in American letters. For immediate experience, however, the diaries, journals, and letters of soldiers on both sides of the fighting—many of them unpublished—provide historians with the most vivid and compelling accounts of the war.

From the sidelines, as it were, the selfless individuals who staffed military medical corps bore witness to the human ravages of war. Among the volunteers were Louisa May Alcott and Walt Whitman, both hospital assistants in Washington, D.C., and authors of first-person reflections on battlefield suffering—hers a collection of letters home published as *Hospital Sketches* (1863), his a series of poems collected in *Drum-Taps* (1865). Canadian-born Sarah Emma Evelyn Edmonds, who dressed as a boy while fighting in the Second Michigan regiment but deserted for fear of revealing her gender, recounted her service after 1863 in *Nurse and Spy in the Union Army* (1865), in which she describes soldiers wounded by shelling "as if smitten by thunderbolts."

As the war drew to a close, Lincoln's second inaugural address of March 4, 1865, joined the ranks of landmark orations in American history. Rather than celebrate the Union triumph, the tired president invoked God's will as the only prevailing power in the conflict. Rather than seek retribution for the defeated South, he called for a pragmatic, reconciliatory approach to Reconstruction—"with malice toward none, with charity for all."

Lincoln's death by an assassin's bullet less than six weeks later brought an outpouring of elegiac writing, including Walt Whitman's canonical poems "O Captain! My Captain!" and "When Lilacs Last in the Dooryard Bloom'd" and James Russell Lowell's "Commemoration Ode," a meditation on the triumph of Unionism and the wisdom of Lincoln—"one of Plutarch's men [who] talked with us face to face"—recited at a Harvard University commemoration on July 21.

Southern Views

Often neglected in the critical history of American letters are the works of Southern writers from the antebellum period through Reconstruction. Perhaps foremost among the prewar voices was that of South Carolina novelist, poet, and critic William Gilmore Simms, whose best-known works are the novels *The Yemassee* (1835) and *The Cassique of Kiawah* (1859), modeled on the realistic style of James Fenimore Cooper. A strong supporter of slavery and the Southern cause, Simms also wrote reviews and a novel, *The Sword and the Distaff* (1852), in response to *Uncle Tom's Cabin.*

Distinguished among personal narratives of antebellum plantation society and Southern civilian life during the war is the diary of Mary Boykin Chesnut, the wife of a Confederate officer who served as a personal aide to President Jefferson Davis. Written from February 1861 to August 1865, Chesnut's journal entries were first published as *A Diary of Dixie* (1905) and later in complete, annotated form as *Mary Chesnut's Civil War* (1981).

Much as in the North, many of the enduring accounts of war from the Southern point of view came from women in a supporting capacity. Nurse Kate Cumming of Mobile, Alabama, published *A Journal of Hospital Life in the Confederate Army in Tennessee* (1866), a memoir of her humble chores in laundry and kitchen and her travail in September 1863 as a nurse at the Battle of Chickamauga. Cornelia Philips accounted for the diminished condition of soldiers in *The Last Ninety Days of the War in North Carolina* (1866), a bitter memoir of thousands of deaths accelerated by shortages of food and medicine. Fannie A. Beers, author of *Memories: A Record of Personal Experiences and Adventures During Four Years of War* (1888), recalled daily portions of mule meat at army messes in Alabama, Georgia, and Virginia. These and other direct accounts honed the era's taste for realism and offered female authors opportunities to publish in a male-dominated market.

The final defeat of the Confederacy gave rise to a regional literary movement that took the name "Lost Cause," characterized by

Many of the enduring accounts of war from the Southern point of view came from women in a supporting capacity.

an enduring belief in the justice and nobility of the Southern cause; a conviction that battlefield losses were strictly the result of Union advantages in weaponry and manpower; and staunch opposition to Reconstruction. Key texts in this new genre were the apologia of military leaders, most notably Robert E. Lee's "Farewell Address to his Soldiers" (General Order No. 9), delivered near Appomattox Court House in April 1865; a series of articles by General Jubal Early for the Southern Historical Society in the 1870s; and Jefferson Davis's two-volume *The Rise and Fall of the Confederate Government* (1881). From Southern women, postwar laments included poems by Charleston, South Carolina, native Caroline August Ball—notably "The Jacket of Gray" (1866)—and a series of articles by former Confederate first lady Varina Howell Davis for the *New York World* in her final years, including a tribute to General Grant and a nostalgic piece titled "Christmas in the Confederate White House" (1896).

Among the brightest lights of Southern Reconstruction literature was the Georgia-born former blockade runner Sidney Lanier, a survivor of the Union's Camp Point Lookout prison in Maryland. Lanier spent the remaining 16 years of his life playing the flute and writing regional verse while fighting "prison lung" (consumption). Immersed in the cadence, dialect, and immediacy of the South, his lyric verse of the outdoors suggested the genial style of Henry David Thoreau. His more mature nature poems, such as "The Symphony" (1875), "The Song of the Chattahoochee" (1877), and "The Marshes of Glynn" (1878), took on a higher luxuriance and grandeur. The haunted phrases of his later work evoked poignant themes of regret, reconciliation, and dread—the assimilation of former secessionists and the growth of industry and urbanism.

Jeff Hacker and Mary Ellen Snodgrass

See also: Abolitionist and Antislavery Movements; Reconstruction; Slavery and Slave Life

Sidelight

The Civil War in Historical Fiction

American literary historians have long observed a cultural oddity pertaining to the single most traumatic and transformational event in the nation's history: The Civil War produced few, if any, major works of fiction that were written during the four years of conflict or based on firsthand experience of it. Periodicals such as *Harper's Weekly* carried regular field reports and short stories, with authentic artwork and photographs. About their volunteer work in military hospitals, Louisa May Alcott and Walt Whitman wrote letters, sketches, and poems that became part of the literary canon. Diaries, memoirs, and autobiographies have provided detailed, often dramatic accounts of life in combat, slavery, planter society, and high office. In prose fiction, Ambrose Bierce would go on to write powerful short stories based on his years of service in the Union army, most notably "An Occurrence at Owl Creek Bridge" (1890),"Chickamauga" (1889), and "The Major's Tale" (1890).

Nevertheless, the Civil War produced no major novels held in the same regard as ones that emerged from other major turning points in U.S. history—Ernest Hemingway's World War I classic *A Farewell to Arms* (1929), for example; or John Steinbeck's iconic work of the Great Depression, *The Grapes of Wrath* (1939); or such World War II standards as James Jones's *From Here to Eternity* (1951), Norman Mailer's *The Naked and the Dead* (1948), and Joseph Heller's *Catch-22* (1961). This is not to suggest that American novelists have shunned the greatest upheaval in the nation's history, nor even that the event did not inspire outstanding works of long fiction. To the contrary, great Civil War novels abound, from the nineteenth to the twenty-first century. A review of major titles, however, does reveal that all are works of *historical fiction*—looking back from a later time without the true sights, sounds, and smells of the battlefield or the anxiety, destruction, or deprivations of the home front in the personal experience of the author.

- *The Red Badge of Courage* (1895), by Stephen Crane. Published 30 years after the end of the war, Crane's novel tells the story of a young Union private who flees in panic from his first battle and then yearns for redemption, in the form of a wound, or "red badge." Although he never actually witnessed combat, Crane re-creates the soldier's experience in naturalistic detail based on veterans' stories and various written accounts.
- *Gone with the Wind* (1936), by Margaret Mitchell: A Pulitzer Prize–winning novel on which the 1939 film classic was based, this historical romance follows Scarlett O'Hara, the spoiled daughter of a Georgia plantation owner, through the loss of the family estate and—as the title suggests—Southern society itself during and after the war.
- *Shiloh: A Novel* (1952), by Shelby Foote: The noted Civil War historian uses first-person fictional narratives to recount the Battle of Shiloh, one of the most brutal of the war, virtually hour by hour from April 6 to 7, 1862.
- *Andersonville* (1955), by MacKinlay Kantor: Journalist and novelist Kantor won the 1956 Pulitzer Prize for Fiction for this novel about the notorious Confederate prisoner of war camp in Andersonville, Georgia. Based in part on the memoirs of actual prisoners, Kantor's story blends the narratives of real and fictional characters.
- *Killer Angels* (1974), by Michael Shaara: Celebrated for its vivid depictions and historical accuracy—especially the motivations, strategies, and moment-by-moment decisions of officers on both sides—Shaara's novel tells the story of the epic Battle of Gettysburg in July 1863. *Killer Angels* also won a Pulitzer Prize for Fiction and was adapted for the big screen (*Gettysburg*, 1993).
- North and South (1980s), by John Jakes: This trilogy of best-selling novels—*North and South* (1982), *Love and War* (1984), and *Heaven and Hell* (1987)—focuses on two families, one in the North and one in the South, before, during, and after the Civil War. Sons from the two families become friends at West Point but find themselves on opposite sides after the fighting breaks out.

- *Beloved* (1987), by Toni Morrison: Not a Civil War novel strictly speaking, Morrison's acclaimed work explores the psychological effects of slavery and emancipation on an African American woman who escapes bondage from Kentucky but faces recapture in Ohio with her four children. A haunting work inspired by a true story, *Beloved* was awarded a Pulitzer Prize for Fiction in 1988.
- *Oldest Living Confederate Widow Tells All* (1989), by Allan Gurganus: From her bed in a rest home, 99-year-old Lucy Marsden recalls her marriage at age 15 to a 50-year-old Civil War veteran who never recovered from the trauma he suffered in the war. Along the way, Marsden offers her unique perspectives on Southern history and society.
- *Gods and Generals* (1996), by Jeff Shaara: A prequel to his father's *Killer Angels,* Jeff Shaara's sweeping novel covers events during the period 1858–1863, leading up to the Battle of Gettysburg and focusing on the lives, characters, and intersecting paths of military leaders on both sides.
- *Cold Mountain* (1997), by Charles Frazier: A wounded Confederate soldier, W.P. Inman, deserts the hospital and begins a long, *Odyssey*-like journey on foot to his home in North Carolina and his beloved, Ada.
- *The March* (2005), by E.L. Doctorow: This award-winning historical novel recreates General William Tecumseh Sherman's march of destruction through Georgia, North Carolina, and South Carolina with 60,000 Union troops in late 1864 and early 1865.
- *March* (2006), by Geraldine Brooks: Paralleling one of the great literary works of the Civil War era, Brooks imagines the wartime experiences of Mr. March—an abolitionist, a chaplain, and the father of the four sisters in Louisa May Alcott's classic children's novel *Little Women* (1868–1869). *March* won the 2006 Pulitzer Prize for Fiction.

Abolitionist and Antislavery Movements

The "peculiar institution" of slavery lay at the heart of America's basic social, political, and economic structures throughout the early republic and antebellum periods. As enslaved labor formed the basis of many white Americans' wealth and social position, resistance to any notion of emancipation was fierce in both the North and the South. Nevertheless, a growing contingent of Americans, white and black, worked to end the institution by forming political parties and antislavery societies, petitioning the government, delivering speeches and sermons, writing books and pamphlets, boycotting slave products, and even organizing slave uprisings. The more radical antislavery activists—abolitionists—argued for an immediate and unconditional end to slavery and racial prejudice in American society. Others espoused antislavery principles but held back from radical abolitionism. These "Free Soilers," as they came to be known, opposed the expansion of slavery but did not call for full emancipation.

Early Resistance to Slavery

The American Revolution sparked debate throughout the new nation as to the true meaning of liberty and the contradictions inherent in a republic that proclaimed "all men are created equal" but that held a significant portion of its population in bondage. In a changing economic climate that made communities in the North less reliant on slavery, several states introduced gradual emancipation laws beginning in the 1780s. Pennsylvania passed the first such law in 1780, followed by Connecticut and Rhode Island in 1784, New York in 1799, and New Jersey in 1804. These laws were gradual in the sense that they offered freedom to enslaved children, but only when they reached adulthood.

Two states abolished slavery outright—Vermont in its first state constitution in 1777 and Massachusetts by judicial ruling in 1783.

Free black communities in the North grew dramatically in the 1790s, with African American leaders such as Richard Allen and Absalom Jones forming independent black churches and other organizations dedicated to combating slavery and discrimination. The states of the Chesapeake Bay region, whose economies were more reliant on slavery than those of the Northern states, did not pass gradual emancipation laws, though Virginia, Delaware, and Maryland did pass laws (in 1782, 1787, and 1790, respectively) that made it easier for owners to manumit (free) their slaves.

The tentative advances in the Chesapeake largely ceased with the advent of the Haitian Revolution in 1791. Alarmed at reports from the French colony of Saint-Domingue (later Haiti) regarding an armed slave uprising, proslavery interests in America began advocating stricter laws regulating the nation's slave population. The unease of white Southerners only increased in 1800, after a planned insurrection by enslaved blacksmith Gabriel Prosser was thwarted in the Richmond, Virginia, area. The legislatures of Virginia and other states responded with laws that further restricted the activities of free blacks as well as slaves.

From Colonization to Radical Abolitionism

Nearly every Northern state emancipated its slaves by 1810, and the few holdouts would fall in line within the next decade. Given the success of gradual emancipation in the North, many Americans concluded that the strategy also would work in the South. Thus, in 1816, supporters of gradual emancipation formed the American Colonization Society (ACS), which advocated that slaves be liberated and sent to the West African colony of Liberia. ACS opposition to slavery was rooted less in a desire to secure racial equality than in a belief that America ought to be a "white man's country," with no African Americans at all. ACS members, both Northern and Southern, felt that African Americans could never be compatible with whites and posed a threat to the safety and well-being of the country by presenting a constant threat of revolt. The racial prejudice underlying the goals of the ACS was not lost on members of the African American community, which was deeply critical of the

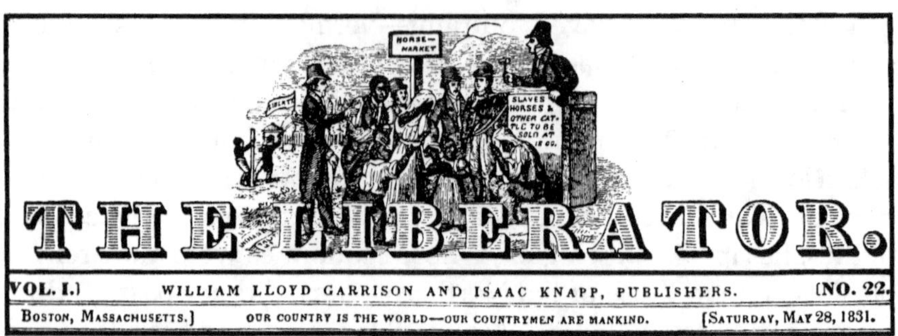

THE LIBERATOR.

VOL. I.] WILLIAM LLOYD GARRISON AND ISAAC KNAPP, PUBLISHERS. [NO. 22.

BOSTON, MASSACHUSETTS.] OUR COUNTRY IS THE WORLD—OUR COUNTRYMEN ARE MANKIND. [SATURDAY, MAY 28, 1831.

William Lloyd Garrison's weekly newspaper *The Liberator* spearheaded the antislavery press from 1831 to 1865, advancing the cause through "moral suasion."

colonization movement from the outset and spoke out consistently against the ACS and its activities. Despite this opposition, the ACS was the preeminent antislavery organization in the United States for two decades after its founding.

Partly in reaction to the colonization movement, advocates of abolitionism began to mobilize during the late 1820s and early 1830s. Members of the Quaker community were early pioneers of the movement, calling on fellow Friends to work for racial equality and to support the Free Produce movement, which discouraged the purchase of any goods produced through slave labor. In 1829, one of the chief architects of the abolitionist movement, African American activist David Walker of Massachusetts, published a pamphlet called *Appeal to the Colored Citizens of the World.* In that tract, Walker urged the black community to take pride in its African heritage and called on slaves to rise up for their freedom. The pamphlet went through three printings in the first year and alarmed many slaveholders. Several Southern states passed laws banning the circulation of abolitionist literature; others passed tighter restrictions on slave life and education.

In 1831, Boston abolitionist William Lloyd Garrison began publishing a weekly called *The Liberator,* which soon became the most influential antislavery publication in the country. Once a supporter of colonization, then of gradual emancipation, Garrison was persuaded by Quakers and others of the need for full, immediate abolition. "I will be as harsh as truth and as uncompromising as justice," he promised readers in the inaugural edition of *The Liberator.* "I am in earnest—I will not equivocate—I will not excuse—I will not retreat a single inch—AND I WILL BE HEARD." Although the weekly started out with meager subscriptions, Garrison indeed made himself heard. The paper attracted more and more readers during the 1830s, the majority of whom were African American, and helped fuel the debate on slavery throughout American society. *The Liberator* and other antislavery publications were successful in advancing the strategy of "moral suasion"—appeals to conscience and calls for nonviolent, nonpolitical resistance—to achieve full, immediate emancipation.

Momentum

On the strength of publications such as these and a range of other organizing activities, the abolitionist movement achieved remarkable growth during the 1830s. In 1833, the nation's first major organization devoted to the cause of abolition and racial equality, the American Anti-Slavery Society (AASS), was formed in Philadelphia. The AASS was dedicated to two primary goals: (1) the immediate, unconditional abolition of slavery; and (2) the securing of equal rights for all African Americans. To advance its goals, the AASS trained abolitionist lecturers, ran petition drives, published a diverse assortment of abolitionist literature, and distributed that literature throughout the country. The AASS also founded local antislavery societies in such cities as Boston, New York, and Philadelphia, as well as many rural areas.

By 1835, more than 200 antislavery societies were operating in the United States. Because few of them accepted women as members, female abolitionists found other means to support the movement. As members of women's auxiliary groups and by individual effort, female abolitionists advanced the cause in vital ways—writing and distributing literature, gathering signatures in petition drives, and raising significant sums of money to fund other initiatives. A number of women served prominently as organizers, speakers, and authors. Female lecturers such as Maria W. Stewart and Angelina and Sarah Grimké attracted large crowds with their abolitionist speeches during the 1830s.

The visibility and aggressiveness of the abolitionist movement in the 1830s produced a backlash against antislavery activists in both the North and the South. White Southerners were especially enraged by a postal campaign that flooded the South with abolitionist literature, convinced that the dissemination of antislavery ideas would incite slave rebellions. Northern opponents of abolition protested antislavery meetings, attacked antislavery speakers, and destroyed the homes, businesses, and churches of free blacks. In 1835, a mob in Boston dragged William Lloyd Garrison through the streets on the end of a rope until supporters came to his rescue. In 1837, a proslavery mob in Illinois fatally shot abolitionist newspaper editor Elijah Lovejoy.

Division

Although abolitionist sentiment gained strength during the 1830s, the movement was less than unified. Abolitionists shared a desire to see slavery brought to an end, but they often disagreed vehemently over how that goal should be accomplished. Two questions were particularly contentious. The first was what role women should play in the movement. The second was whether slavery could be conquered only by working within the political system.

Living in a society that regarded a woman's proper place as in the home, female abolitionists who engaged in public forms of activism often faced hostility and criticism, from within the movement as well as from opponents. After Abby Kelley became the first woman elected to the business committee of the AASS in 1840, a group of abolitionists opposed to women in leadership positions broke away from the society to form a rival organization, the American and Foreign Anti-Slavery Society (AFASS). Although Kelley's nomination certainly precipitated the rift, a number of other factors contributed to the breakup of the AASS. Members who joined the splinter AFASS had long disagreed with the ideas of AASS leader Garrison, who not only supported women's rights but also advocated pacifism, decried traditional Christianity, and rejected the movement's involvement in politics.

In 1840, supporters of the AFASS formed the first abolitionist political party in the United States, the Liberty Party. The party ran candidates in the presidential elections of 1840 and 1844 but attracted only a small following; it had better success in electing local officials. The Liberty Party dissolved in 1848, and its supporters, along with antislavery Whigs and Democrats, formed the Free Soil Party, which opposed the spread of slavery to new U.S. territories without advocating abolition. The Free Soilers attracted considerably more support in national political contests, in large part because their stance on slavery was less radical.

Violence, Politics, and Literature

In 1850, Congress passed the Fugitive Slave Law, which required that slaves who escaped to the North be returned to their owners in the South; anyone who assisted a runaway was subject to severe penalties. Incensed at the legislation, abolitionist author Harriet Beecher Stowe of Ohio wrote the antislavery novel *Uncle Tom's Cabin,* which she serialized in the Washington, D.C., newspaper *The National Era* in 1851 and 1852, and had published as a book in late 1852. *Uncle Tom's Cabin* was a phenomenal success, selling 10,000 copies within a week and 300,000 copies within a year of publication. Its heart-rending narrative dramatized the case against slavery and fired abolitionist sentiment throughout the Northern states.

Although enforcement of the Fugitive Slave Law resulted in the capture and return of countless runaway slaves, many abolitionists actively resisted slave catchers or otherwise abetted the escape of men, women, and children from bondage. Harriet Tubman, Levi Coffin, and the Reverend John Rankin were only a few of the most active "conductors" in helping escaped slaves make their way to freedom on the Underground Railroad—an informal, covert network of antislavery activists who offered safe haven, food, and connections to runaways en route to the Northern states or Canada.

The Fugitive Slave Law also triggered violent confrontations between abolitionists and slave catchers. In 1854, for example, abolitionists who opposed the return of escaped slave Anthony Burns attempted to free him from the Massachusetts courtroom in which his case was being tried; their efforts failed, and one of Burns's guards was killed in the struggle. Former slave Frederick Douglass spoke for many abolitionists when he declared that the Fugitive Slave Law made him question his support for a strictly pacifist abolitionism. "The only way to make the Fugitive Slave Law a dead letter," Douglass declared, "is to make half a dozen or more dead kidnappers."

Douglass's autobiography, *Narrative of the Life of Frederick Douglass, an American Slave* (1845), was among several books by former slaves that stoked the flames of abolitionism, along with antislavery pamphlets, newspapers, and Stowe's novel. Also notable in the literary genre of the "slave narrative" were the *Narrative of William Wells Brown, a Fugitive Slave* (1847), *Narrative of the Life of Henry Box Brown* (1849), and Harriet Jacobs's *Incidents in the Life of a Slave Girl* (1861), among others.

Farther west, meanwhile, in the Kansas Territory, antislavery activists became involved in a violent struggle during the mid-1850s. In 1854, Congress passed the Kansas-Nebraska Act, which declared that settlers would vote to determine whether or not the territory would allow slavery. As pro- and antislavery settlers poured into the region, bloody conflicts erupted between the two factions. Sympathy for the antislavery cause there grew throughout the North, with the press reporting on the activities of "Border Ruffians" who used violence and intimidation to prevent antislavery settlers from voting in local elections.

The violence over slavery even spilled into the nation's capital. On May 22, 1856, abolitionist senator Charles Sumner of Massachusetts was badly beaten by Representative Preston Brooks of South Carolina shortly after Sumner delivered a controversial antislavery speech about Kansas, in which he insulted Brooks's uncle, South Carolina senator Andrew P. Butler. While many Southerners endorsed Brooks's actions as a legitimate defense of Southern honor, most in the North were horrified by the attack.

The spread of antislavery sentiment during the mid-1850s also gave rise to the new Republican Party in 1854. Abolitionists tended to regard the new party with suspicion, as most Republican leaders opposed the extension of slavery but were unwilling to advocate full emancipation. But party rhetoric about the need to defend the rights of free people from the "Slave Power" proved popular with the Northern public, and the Republican candidate for president in 1856, John C. Frémont, garnered an impressive 33 percent of the popular vote.

The U.S. Supreme Court gave abolitionists new cause for outrage in 1857, when it ruled in the case of *Dred Scott v. Sandford* that no African American, enslaved or free, could be considered a citizen of the United States. Much like the Fugitive Slave Law, the *Dred Scott* decision was profoundly unpopular in the North and strengthened public opinion against slavery. In October 1859, two years after the high court's ruling, white abolitionist John Brown and a group of supporters seized the federal arsenal at Harpers Ferry, Virginia (now West Virginia), hoping their actions would spark a slave rebellion that spread across the South. Federal troops retook the arsenal within two days, and Brown and his men all were captured or killed. To many abolitionists, however, Brown was a hero. Even those who opposed the use of force praised him for his devotion to the cause and his selfless efforts to liberate the enslaved. After his execution that December, Brown was widely eulogized in the North as a martyr to the cause of liberty.

Although abolitionists generally remained ambivalent about the Republican Party, opponents of slavery strongly supported Abraham Lincoln, the party's candidate for president in 1860. After his election precipitated the outbreak of the Civil War in April 1861, abolitionists devoted their energies to ensuring that the conflict was not only a war to defend the Union but also a war to bring slavery to an end. The Emancipation Proclamation of 1863, followed by the Thirteenth Amendment in 1865, made certain that was the case.

Holly M. Kent

See also: Douglass, Frederick; Garrison, William Lloyd; Slavery and Slave Life; Stowe, Harriet Beecher; Underground Railroad

Alcott, Louisa May

(1832–1888)

Author and social activist Louisa May "Lu" Alcott, whose nearly 300 books, stories, and poems include the classic children's novel *Little Women* (two volumes, 1868 and 1869), was also an active campaigner for abolition and woman suffrage.

A native of Germantown, Pennsylvania, she was born on November 29, 1832, to Transcendentalist philosopher, educational reformer, and abolitionist Amos Bronson Alcott and social worker Abigail "Abby" May Alcott. Like the main characters in *Little Women*, she was one of four sisters. The family moved to Boston when she was 6 years old and moved again when she was 12 to the Hillside (later the Wayside), a large home in nearby Concord, Massachusetts. It was there that she began writing and lived many of the scenes that would appear in her popular children's novel. An outbuilding on the property, connected to the main house by tunnel, provided shelter for fugitive slaves on the Underground Railroad.

Taught by their father, Alcott and her sisters were raised in the company of his fellow intellectuals, such as Ralph Waldo Emerson, Margaret Fuller, Julia Ward Howe, James Russell Lowell, Elizabeth Peabody, and Henry David Thoreau, who became her private tutor. From her parents and uncle, the Reverend Samuel Joseph May, cofounder of the American Anti-Slavery Society, she learned the principles of civil rights, libertarianism, and educational reform. At an early age, she displayed a vivid imagination and a talent for writing, which her father encouraged. She published her first poem at age 16.

Early Writings

Despite the intellectual wealth of her upbringing, the family lived in almost constant penury; Alcott resolved to become a successful writer as well as an advocate for social causes. She remained unmarried throughout her adult life, devoting herself to writing and activism. As a teenager, she worked with her older sister Anna as a caregiver for the elderly, housekeeper, and seamstress, and then as a tutor, memoirist, fiction writer, playwright, and editor of the children's magazine *Merry's Museum.* Under "L.M. Alcott" and other gender-neutral pen names, she freelanced for the *American Union, Atlantic Monthly, Flag of Our Union, Frank Leslie's Chimney Corner, Peterson's Magazine,* and *The Woman's Journal,* a suffragist publication edited by Lucy Stone. Alcott published her first book, a collection of children's stories titled *Flower Fables,* in 1854. In addition, she wrote essays on slavery, the boycott of slave-made goods, women's rights, and, later, temperance.

In May and June 1863, with the Civil War raging for more than two years, the abolitionist magazine *Boston Commonwealth* published Alcott's letters home from Union Hospital, a converted hotel and tavern on Thirtieth Street in Washington, D.C., where she had volunteered in December 1862 as a ward nurse for the U.S. Sanitary Commission. Her duties in the dank, gangrene-smelling hospital included bathing and dosing wounded Union soldiers, cleaning and re-bandaging their wounds, soothing their pain, and writing notes on their behalf. Although she admitted, "I indulged in a most unpatriotic wish that I was safe at home again," she accepted promotion to night duty and continued serving for two months. Her wartime letters were later published in book form as *Hospital Sketches* (1863).

In Washington in February 1863, Alcott fell ill with typhoid. Fever reduced her to delirium for three weeks and required the shaving of her long brown hair. Treatment of her fever, aching limbs, and ulcerated throat with mercury-laced calomel caused hallucinations and flashbacks, which pursued her on the train ride home through New York. When her strength returned, she wrote the romance novel *Pauline's Passion and Punishment* (1863), published under the pseudonym A.M. Barnard. She would go on to write a succession of lucrative Gothic novels, melodramas, and what she called "lurid tales" for magazines, all published anonymously or under pen names. Book-length works included *The Marble Woman* (1865), *The Abbot's Ghost* (1867), *Behind a Mask* (1875), and *A Modern Mephistopheles* (1877). A number of romantic stories and novellas went unidentified as Alcott's work until the 1970s.

Louisa May Alcott, best known as the author of the children's novel *Little Women* (1868), won her first literary acclaim for accounts of her work as a ward nurse in a Civil War hospital.

Children's Writer and Proto-Feminist

Despite the positive critical response to her war correspondence and the commercial success of her romance fiction, it was as a writer of children's and domestic literature that Alcott finally achieved the literary success to which she aspired. The breakthrough came in October 1868 with the publication of the first volume of her semiautobiographical novel *Little Women,* about the joys and sacrifices of four sisters—Meg, Jo (Alcott's alter ego), Beth, and Amy March—growing up in a financially strapped middle-class family in mid-nineteenth-century New England. After selling more than 60,000 copies in the first year, she released a second volume in 1869, titled *Good Wives,* which followed the sisters into adulthood and marriage. The two volumes were published as a single work, titled *Little Women,* for the first time in 1880. Meanwhile, Alcott had produced a sequel, *Little Men,* in 1871, followed by *Jo's Boys* in 1886, about the next generation of March children.

Modern literary critics have pointed to a distinct proto-feminist strain in *Little Women,* with Jo and her sisters portraying a strong female identity tempered with sisterhood, self-sacrifice, and compassion. Alcott continued her woman-centered bent with *An Old-Fashioned Girl* (1870) as well as *Little Men* and *Eight Cousins,* issued serially in 1874–1875. The latter provided insight into New England family life, morality, and the home training and education of girls during and after the Civil War.

Increasingly during the antebellum era, Alcott acknowledged the similarity between the plights of African Americans and women in America. In her semiautobiographical novel *Work: A Story of Experience* (1873) and its sequel, *Beginning Again* (1875), she makes the case for female cooperation and mutual respect as the foundation of equality and social justice in women's lives. And in a treatise titled *Moods* (1882), she urged women to take charge of their destiny: "The duty we owe ourselves is greater than that we owe [others]," she wrote.

In 1877, Alcott joined physician Harriet Winifred Clisby, Unitarian teacher Abby Morton Diaz, reformer Mary Thorn Lewis Gannett, and writer Julia Ward Howe in founding the Women's Educational and Industrial Union, an outreach organization in Boston that offered employment, medical care, and legal aid to poor female laborers. In 1878, she became the first woman in Concord to register to vote.

Alcott fought chronic health problems in her later years, perhaps the result of the mercury treatments she had received as a young woman. She continued to write until her death, on March 6, 1888. More than a century later, in 1995, her Gothic suspense novel *A Long Fatal Love Chase,* written in 1866 under the name A.M. Barnard, was published for the first time.

Mary Ellen Snodgrass

See also: Abolitionist and Antislavery Movements

Hospital Sketches (excerpt), 1863

In 1863, five years before the publication of her classic children's novel Little Women, *Louisa May Alcott earned her first literary acclaim for a series of articles that appeared in* Boston Commonwealth *magazine and were based on her letters home during a two-month stint as a Civil War nurse at Union Hospital in Washington, D.C. The experiences recounted below follow the arrival of 40 ambulances from the Battle of Fredericksburg on Christmas Day, 1862.*

The sight of several stretchers, each with its legless, armless, or desperately wounded occupant, entering my ward, admonished me that I was there to work, not to wonder or weep; so I corked up my feelings, and returned to the path of duty, which was rather "a hard road to travel" just then. The house had been a hotel before hospitals were needed, and many of the doors still bore their old names; some not so inappropriate as might be imagined, for my ward was in truth a *ball-room,* if gun-shot wounds could christen it. Forty beds were prepared, many already tenanted by tired men who fell down anywhere, and drowsed till the smell of food roused them. Round the great stove was gathered the dreariest group I ever saw—ragged, gaunt and pale, mud to the knees, with bloody bandages untouched since put on days before; many bundled up in blankets, coats being lost or useless; and all wearing that disheartened look which proclaimed defeat, more plainly than any telegram of the Burnside blunder. I pitied them so much, I dared not speak to them, though, remembering all they had been through since the route at Fredericksburg, I yearned to serve the dreariest of them all. Presently, Miss Blank tore me from my refuge behind piles of one-sleeved shirts, odd socks, bandages and lint; put basin, sponge, towels, and a block of brown soap into my hands, with these appalling directions:

"Come, my dear, begin to wash as fast as you can. Tell them to take off socks, coats and shirts, scrub them well, put on clean shirts, and the attendants will finish them off, and lay them in bed."

If she had requested me to shave them all, or dance a hornpipe on the stove funnel, I should have been less staggered; but to scrub some dozen lords of creation at a moment's notice, was really–really–. However, there was no time for nonsense, and, having resolved when I came to do everything I was bid, I drowned my scruples in my wash-bowl, clutched my soap manfully, and, assuming a business-like air, made a dab at the first dirty specimen I saw, bent on performing my task *vi et armis* if necessary. I chanced to light on a withered old Irishman, wounded in the head, which caused that portion of his frame to be tastefully laid out like a garden, the bandages being the walks, his hair the shrubbery. He was so overpowered by the honor of having a lady wash him, as he expressed it, that he did nothing but roll up his eyes, and bless me, in an irresistible style which was too much for my sense of the ludicrous; so we laughed together, and when I knelt down to take off his shoes, he "flopped" also, and wouldn't hear of my touching "them dirty craters. May your bed above be aisy darlin,' for the day's work ye ar doon!–Whoosh! there ye are, and bedad, it's hard tellin' which is the dirtiest, the fut or the shoe." It was; and if he hadn't been to the fore, I should have gone on pulling, under the impression that the "fut" was a boot, for trousers, socks, shoes and legs were a mass of mud. This comical tableau produced a general grin, at which propitious beginning I took heart and scrubbed away like any tidy parent on a Saturday night. Some of them took the performance like sleepy children, leaning their tired heads against me as I worked, others looked grimly scandalized, and several of the roughest colored like bashful girls. One wore a soiled little bag about his neck, and, as I moved it, to bathe his wounded breast, I said,

"Your talisman didn't save you, did it?"

"Well, I reckon it did, marm, for that shot would a gone a couple a inches deeper but for my old mammy's camphor bag," answered the cheerful philosopher.

Another, with a gun-shot wound through the cheek, asked for a looking-glass, and when I brought one, regarded his swollen face with a dolorous expression, as he muttered—"I vow to gosh, that's too bad! I warn't a bad looking chap before, and now I'm done for; won't there be a thunderin' scar? and what on earth will Josephine Skinner say?"

He looked up at me with his one eye so appealingly, that I controlled my risibles, and assured him that if Josephine was a girl of sense, she would admire the honorable scar, as a lasting proof that he had faced the enemy, for all women thought a wound the best decoration a brave soldier could wear. I hope Miss Skinner verified the good opinion I so rashly expressed of her, but I shall never know.

The next scrubbee was a nice looking lad, with a curly brown mane, and a budding trace of gingerbread over the lip, which he called his beard, and defended stoutly, when the barber jocosely suggested its immolation. He lay on a bed, with one leg gone, and the right arm so shattered that it must evidently follow: yet the little Sergeant was as merry as if his afflictions were not worth lamenting over; and when a drop or two of salt water mingled with my suds at the sight of this strong young body, so marred and maimed, the boy looked up, with a brave smile, though there was a little quiver of the lips, as he said,

Another, with a gun-shot wound through the cheek, asked for a looking-glass, and when I brought one, regarded his swollen face with a dolorous expression.

"Now don't you fret yourself about me, miss; I'm first rate here, for it's nuts to lie still on this bed, after knocking about in those confounded ambulances, that shake what there is left of a fellow to jelly. I never was in one of these places before, and think this cleaning up a jolly thing for us, though I'm afraid it isn't for you ladies."

"Is this your first battle, Sergeant?"

"No, miss; I've been in six scrimmages, and never got a scratch till this last one; but it's done the business pretty thoroughly for me, I should say. Lord! what a scramble there'll be for arms and legs, when we old boys come out of our graves, on the Judgment Day: wonder if we shall get our own again? If we do, my leg will have to tramp from Fredericksburg, my arm from here, I suppose, and meet my body, wherever it may be."

The fancy seemed to tickle him mightily, for he laughed blithely, and so did I; which, no doubt, caused the new nurse to be regarded as a light-minded sinner by the Chaplain, who roamed vaguely about, informing the men that they were all worms, corrupt of heart, with perishable bodies, and souls only to be saved by a diligent perusal of certain tracts, and other equally cheering bits of spiritual consolation, when spirituous ditto would have been preferred. . . .

Having done up our human wash, and laid it out to dry, the second syllable of our version of the word war-fare was enacted with much success. Great trays of bread, meat, soup and coffee appeared; and both nurses and attendants turned waiters, serving bountiful rations to all who could eat. I can call my pinafore to testify to my good will in the work, for in ten minutes it was reduced to a perambulating bill of fare, presenting samples of all the refreshments going or gone. It was a lively scene; the long room lined with rows of beds, each filled by an occupant, whom water, shears, and clean raiment, had transformed from a dismal ragamuffin into a recumbent hero, with a cropped head. To and fro rushed matrons, maids, and convalescent "boys," skirmishing with knives and forks; retreating with empty plates; marching and counter-marching, with unvaried success. . . .

Very welcome seemed the generous meal, after a week of suffering, exposure, and short commons; soon the brown faces began to smile, as food, warmth, and rest, did their pleasant work; and the grateful "Thankee's" were followed by more graphic accounts of the battle and retreat, than any paid reporter could have given us. Curious contrasts of the tragic and comic met one everywhere; and some touching as well as ludicrous episodes, might have been recorded that day. A six foot New Hampshire man, with a leg broken and perforated by a piece of shell, so large that, had I not seen the wound, I should have regarded the story as a Munchausenism, beckoned me to come and help him, as he could not sit up, and both his bed and beard were getting plentifully anointed with soup. As I fed my big nestling with corresponding mouthfuls, I asked him how he felt during the battle.

"Well, 'twas my fust, you see, so I aint ashamed to say I was a trifle flustered in the beginnin,' there was such an allfired racket; for ef there's anything I do spleen agin, it's noise. But when my mate, Eph Sylvester, caved, with a bullet through his head, I got mad, and pitched in, licketty cut. Our part of the fight didn't last long; so a lot of us larked round Fredericksburg, and give some of them houses a pretty consid'able of a rummage, till we was ordered out of the mess. Some of our fellows cut like time; but I warn't a-goin' to run for nobody; and, fust thing I knew, a shell bust, right in front of us, and I keeled over, feelin' as if I was blowed higher'n a kite. I sung out, and the boys come back for me, double quick; but the way they chucked me over them fences was a caution, I tell you. Next day I was most as black as that darkey yonder, lickin' plates on the sly. This is bully coffee, ain't it? Give us another pull at it, and I'll be obleeged to you."

I did; and, as the last gulp subsided, he said, with a rub of his old handkerchief over eyes as well as mouth:

"Look a here; I've got a pair a earbobs and a handkercher pin I'm a goin' to give you, if you'll have them; for you're the very moral o' Lizy Sylvester, poor Eph's wife: that's why I signalled you to come over here. They aint much, I guess, but they'll do to memorize the rebs by."

Burrowing under his pillow, he produced a little bundle of what he called "truck," and gallantly presented me with a pair of earrings, each representing a cluster of corpulent grapes, and the pin a basket of astonishing fruit, the whole large and coppery enough for a small warming-pan. Feeling delicate about depriving him of such valuable relics, I accepted the earrings alone, and was obliged to depart, somewhat abruptly, when my friend stuck the warming-pan in the bosom of his night-gown, viewing it with much complacency, and, perhaps, some tender memory, in that rough heart of his, for the comrade he had lost.

Observing that the man next him had left his meal untouched, I offered the same service I had performed for his neighbor, but he shook his head.

"Thank you, ma'am; I don't think I'll ever eat again, for I'm shot in the stomach. But I'd like a drink of water, if you aint too busy."

I rushed away, but the water-pails were gone to be refilled, and it was some time before they reappeared. I did not forget my patient patient, meanwhile, and, with the first mugful, hurried back to him. He seemed asleep; but something in the tired white face caused me to listen at his lips for a breath. None came. I touched his forehead; it was cold: and then I knew that, while he waited, a better nurse than I had given him a cooler draught, and healed him with a touch. I laid the sheet over the quiet sleeper, whom no noise could now disturb; and, half an hour later, the bed was empty. It seemed a poor requital for all he had sacrificed and suffered,–that hospital bed, lonely even in a crowd; for there was no familiar face for him to look his last upon; no friendly voice to say, Good bye; no hand to lead him gently down into the Valley of the Shadow; and he vanished, like a drop in that red sea upon whose shores so many women stand lamenting. For a moment I felt bitterly indignant at this seeming carelessness of the value of life, the sanctity of death; then consoled myself with the thought that, when the great muster roll was called, these nameless men might be promoted above many whose tall monuments record the barren honors they have won.

Sources: Digital Library, University of Pennsylvania (http://digital.library.upenn.edu); Louisa May Alcott, *Hospital Sketches* (Boston: James Redpath, 1863).

Chesnut, Mary

(1823–1886)

Capturing both the panic and stoicism of the civilian population in all social classes, diarist Mary Boykin Miller Chesnut of South Carolina provided a unique portrait of Southern society before and during the Civil War. As the wife of a Confederate officer who was also a personal aide to President Jefferson Davis, Chesnut could describe the interactions among Southern elites and the major developments of the war from a unique vantage point. Her diary, covering the period February 1861 to August 1865 (but not published until 1905), is regarded by scholars as perhaps the greatest literary accomplishment of the Confederacy.

Early Life

Born on March 31, 1823, in Stateburg, South Carolina, she was the eldest of four children of Stephen Decatur Miller, a governor and U.S. senator from that state, and Mary Boykin. She also bore the name of her maternal grandmother, Mary Whitaker Boykin, a matriarch of the Southern aristocracy.

The future diarist learned reading from her paternal grandmother, Margaret Moore White Miller, and basic writing skills at a day school several miles away in Camden. In the fall of 1835, at age 12, she began studying French, German, history, literature, music, rhetoric, and science at Madame Talvande's French School for Young Ladies, an elite academy in the heart of Charleston. Spending periods between school terms on a family estate in Mississippi, the girl developed sympathy for the plight of black slaves and wondered how bondage could be accepted as a harmless institution. At age 17, she married attorney James Chesnut, Jr., a future U.S. senator (1857–1862) and the son of a large South Carolina plantation owner; the couple moved into a three-story mansion in Camden called Kamchatka.

Active on the entertainment circuit of upper-crust planter society, Mary Chesnut nevertheless suffered bouts of depression and marital discord. At the heart of her discontent, aside from an inability to have children, lay a resentment of patriarchy—including that of her husband, whose career moves determined her destiny. On the eve of war, the Chesnuts settled in Charleston while James served as aide-de-camp to Confederate general P.G.T. Beauregard. On April 12, 1861, while staying at the John Rutledge household on Battery Row, Mary observed the predawn Confederate cannonade on Fort Sumter and knelt to pray for the South.

On April 23, she retreated to Mulberry Plantation, the Chesnut homestead on the Wateree River south of Camden, but she continued to receive reports on Charleston, where privateers breached the Union blockade. Based on her assessment of Southern war production and what she had heard about military installations, she believed that Confederate coastal defenses would hold against the Union. Her faith wavered on December 13, 1861, when a fire of suspicious origin consumed Charleston from East Bay down Broad Street, river to river.

War's Specter

With her frequent moves and daily reading of the press from Charleston, New York, Richmond, and Washington, D.C., Chesnut acquired a liberal view of the South's ruin. While her husband served as chief of staff to Confederate president Jefferson Davis in Richmond, she befriended first lady Varina Howell Davis.

The diarist's dozen volumes summarized the end of slavery and the funerals of relatives and friends killed in the conflict. Beyond writing, Chesnut responded actively to those in need. To patients at a Charlottesville hospital infected with typhoid fever, she sent a supply of white sugar. In late August 1861, while at Robertson Hospital in Richmond, she delivered peaches and grapes to Captain Sally Louisa Tompkins, the only woman holding an officer's rank in the Confederate army. While fever—probably malaria—kept Chesnut housebound for part of 1862, she reported in her diary on military scuttlebutt and the snobbery within Charleston women's auxiliaries, which the upper crust left to lower-class females. From August 1862 to October 1863, she was too busy as a volunteer feeder of wounded soldiers in Columbia Junction to keep up her journal.

Fearing a Union invasion, Chesnut kept luggage packed for retreat to safer inland locations. Meanwhile, she poured out her opinions in daily retrospectives. She railed against antislavery author Harriet Beecher Stowe as a Northern agitator, disapproved of the concubinage of females by white slave owners, and grieved over the pillage at Mulberry. By 1864, with Southern rail service at a halt, she held out little hope of a Confederate triumph. With the currency devalued and society disintegrating all around her, she partnered with her maid Molly in selling butter and eggs to generate cash. On February 16, 1865, during the march across the South by Union general Tecumseh Sherman and just weeks before the fall of Richmond, Chesnut fled Columbia and hurried by train through Charlotte, North Carolina, to the relative safety of Lincolnton.

Reduced Circumstance

Dislocation tested Chesnut's ability to cope. In North Carolina, she paid the enormous sum of $30 a day for squalid accommodations and lived on the contents of a food box packed with coffee, flour, rice, and sugar. With Sherman's army having devastated homes and fields across the South, and with Yankee carpetbaggers now occupying South Carolina, Chesnut lapsed into hysterical weeping at the fate of her family and way of life. Among streams of displaced persons, she accepted handouts of chicken, preserves, and sausages from friends. Finally in mid-March 1865, she was able to move back to South Carolina and reunite with James at a three-room residence in Chester. In the weeks that followed, the Chesnut house became a magnet for elite Southern refugees—including first lady Varina Davis and her four children—who bedded down on pallets. On August 2, Mary made her final journal entry.

After the war, with husband James Chesnut resuming his law practice and political career, the return of former slaves and displacement of kin increased Mary's responsibility as a plantation mistress. But Reconstruction reduced the Chesnuts to penury. At Sarsfield, their estate built in 1873, she lived on $100 a year plus $144 from the sale of dairy goods and eggs. Varina Davis, recognizing the strain on Chesnut's failing heart, urged her to support herself by publishing the war diaries.

In 1881, Chesnut began reorganizing the 460 notebooks of her journal—an endeavor that would continue for five years—and submitted one episode, "The Arrest of a Spy," to the *Charleston Weekly News and Courier.* Her financial situation worsened after James's death in February 1885, as his estate was riddled with debt and he left the plantation to a male heir. Mary Chesnut died of heart disease on November 22, 1886. An abridged version of her journal, titled *A Diary of Dixie,* was published in 1905. A more complete, annotated version in 1981, *Mary Chesnut's Civil War* (1981), earned editor C. Vann Woodward a Pulitzer Prize for history.

Mary Ellen Snodgrass

A Diary of Dixie (excerpt), 1861

The diary of Mary Boykin Chesnut, the wife of a Confederate officer and top aide to President Jefferson Davis, provides a vivid account of the unfolding of the Civil War and how it affected Southern society. Beginning at her plantation in Charleston, South Carolina, and throughout her peregrinations during the war—she accompanied her husband to many of its most significant locations—Chesnut kept her journal from February 1861 to August 1865. The entries that follow, from the 1905 edition, describe the Union bombardment of Fort Sumter in Charleston Harbor—the opening salvos of the Civil War in April 1861—as seen from the nearby rooftops and experienced by the Chesnuts and their acquaintances.

April 12th. Anderson will not capitulate. Yesterday's was the merriest, maddest dinner we have had yet. Men were audaciously wise and witty. We had an unspoken foreboding that it was to be our last pleasant meeting. Mr. Miles dined with us to-day. Mrs. Henry King rushed in saying, "The news, I come for the latest news. All the men of the King family are on the Island," of which fact she seemed proud.

While she was here our peace negotiator, or envoy, came in—that is, Mr. Chesnut returned. His interview with Colonel

Anderson had been deeply interesting, but Mr. Chesnut was not inclined to be communicative. He wanted his dinner. He felt for Anderson and had telegraphed to President Davis for instructions—what answer to give Anderson, etc. He has now gone back to Fort Sumter with additional instructions. When they were about to leave the wharf A.H. Boykin sprang into the boat in great excitement. He thought himself ill-used, with a likelihood of fighting and he to be left behind!

I do not pretend to go to sleep. How can I? If Anderson does not accept terms at four, the orders are, he shall be fired upon. I count four, St. Michael's bells chime out and I begin to hope. At half-past four the heavy booming of a cannon. I sprang out of bed, and on my knees prostrate I prayed as I never prayed before.

There was a sound of stir all over the house, pattering of feet in the corridors. All seemed hurrying one way. I put on my double-gown and a shawl and went, too. It was to the housetop. The shells were bursting. In the dark I heard a man say, "Waste of ammunition." I knew my husband was rowing about in a boat somewhere in that dark bay, and that the shells were roofing it over, bursting toward the fort. If Anderson was obstinate, Colonel Chesnut was to order the fort on one side to open fire. Certainly fire had begun. The regular roar of the cannon, there it was. And who could tell what each volley accomplished of death and destruction?

The women were wild there on the housetop. Prayers came from the women and imprecations from the men. And then a shell would light up the scene. To-night they say the forces are to attempt to land. We watched up there, and everybody wondered that Fort Sumter did not fire a shot.

To-day Miles and Manning, colonels now, aides to Beauregard, dined with us. The latter hoped I would keep the peace. I gave him only good words, for he was to be under fire all day and night, down in the bay carrying orders, etc.

Last night, or this morning truly, up on the housetop I was so weak and weary I sat down on something that looked like a black stool. "Get up, you foolish woman. Your dress is on fire," cried a man. And he put me out. I was on a chimney and the sparks had caught my clothes. Susan Preston and Mr. Venable then came up. But my fire had been extinguished before it burst out into a regular blaze.

The regular roar of the cannon, there it was. And who could tell what each volley accomplished of death and destruction?

Do you know, after all that noise and our tears and prayers, nobody has been hurt; sound and fury signifying nothing—a delusion and a snare.

Louisa Hamilton came here now. This is a sort of news center. Jack Hamilton, her handsome young husband, has all the credit of a famous battery, which is made of railroad iron. Mr. Petigru calls it the boomerang, because it throws the balls back the way they came; so Lou Hamilton tells us. During her first marriage, she had no children; hence the value of this lately achieved baby. To divert Louisa from the glories of "the Battery," of which she raves, we asked if the baby could talk yet. "No, not exactly, but he imitates the big gun when he hears that. . . .

Somebody came in just now and reported Colonel Chesnut asleep on the sofa in General Beauregard's room. After two such nights he must be so tired as to be able to sleep anywhere.

Just bade farewell to Langdon Cheves. He is forced to go home and leave this interesting place. Says he feels like the man that was not killed at Thermopylae. I think he said that unfortunate had to hang himself when he got home for very shame. Maybe he fell on his sword, which was the strictly classic way of ending matters.

I do not wonder at Louisa Hamilton's baby; we hear nothing, can listen to nothing; boom, boom goes the cannon all the time. The nervous strain is awful, alone in this darkened room. "Richmond and Washington ablaze," say the papers—blazing with excitement. Why not? To us these last days' events seem frightfully great. We were all women on that iron balcony. Men are only seen at a distance now. Stark Means, marching under the piazza at the head of his regiment, held his cap in his hand all the time he was in sight. Mrs. Means was leaning over and looking with tearful eyes, when an unknown creature asked,

"Why did he take his hat off?" Mrs. Means stood straight up and said: "He did that in honor of his mother; he saw me." She is a proud mother, and at the same time most unhappy. Her lovely daughter Emma is dying in there, before her eyes, of consumption. At that moment I am sure Mrs. Means had a spasm of the heart; at least, she looked as I feel sometimes. She took my arm and we came in.

April 13th. Nobody has been hurt after all. How gay we were last night. Reaction after the dread of all the slaughter we thought those dreadful cannon were making. Not even a battery the worse for wear. Fort Sumter has been on fire. Anderson has not yet silenced any of our guns. So the aides, still with swords and red sashes by way of uniform, tell us. But the sound of those guns makes regular meals impossible. None of us go to table. Tea-trays pervade the corridors going everywhere. Some of the anxious hearts lie on their beds and moan in solitary misery. Mrs. Wigfall and I solace ourselves with tea in my room. These women have all a satisfying faith. "God is on our side," they say. When we are shut in Mrs. Wigfall and I ask "Why?" "Of course, He hates the Yankees, we are told. You'll think that well of Him."

Not by one word or look can we detect any change in the demeanor of these negro servants. Lawrence sits at our door, sleepy and respectful, and profoundly indifferent. So are they all, but they carry it too far. You could not tell that they even heard the awful roar going on in the bay, though it has been dinning in their ears night and day. People talk before them as if they were chairs and tables. They make no sign. Are they stolidly stupid? or wiser than we are; silent and strong, biding their time?

Source: Documenting the American South, the University of North Carolina at Chapel Hill (http://docsouth.unc.edu).

Dickinson, Emily

(1830–1886)

Introverted, enigmatic, and isolated from the outside world for much of her life, Emily Dickinson of Amherst, Massachusetts, crafted delicate but intensely felt verse that was largely untouched by the social, political, or philosophical issues of the times but that illuminated a deep, wide-ranging inner experience with exquisite skill, in a highly original style. While her poems bore little direct relation to the conflict over slavery raging in the nation at large, the emergence of the individual voice and spirit in her verse parallels the fight for individual human freedom at the heart of the antislavery movement. Although Dickinson's work was virtually unknown during her lifetime—only about 10 of her poems are believed to have been published before her death—the "belle of Amherst" would gain standing as one of the two foremost American poets of the nineteenth century, with Walt Whitman.

Emily Elizabeth Dickinson was born on December 10, 1830, in the family homestead on Main Street built by her grandfather, one of the founders of Amherst College. She would spend most of her 55 years as a spinster in that western Massachusetts town.

Of New England Puritan stock, she developed verbal virtuosity and an affinity for music as a toddler. Dominated by an unaffectionate mother, Emily Norcross Dickinson, and a grim Calvinist father, U.S. legislator Edward Dickinson, she was a bright, obedient, but melancholic child. Except from her older brother William, she received little male approval for her poetry and gardening, at which she excelled. In a poem at midlife, "They shut me up in Prose" (ca. 1862), she wrote of her childhood and Victorian upbringing:

when a little Girl
They put me in the Closet—
Because they liked me "still"

Dickinson received an intensive classical education at Amherst Academy, where she spent seven years (1840–1847), and then at the nearby Mount Holyoke Female Seminary. But she returned home from the latter institution after only a year, recoiling from efforts to persuade her to join the Congregational Church. With a distaste for evangelical zeal and the Calvinist principle of predestination, she suffered bouts of depression and fears of death and damnation. Steeped in the Transcendentalism of Ralph Waldo Emerson and its affirmation of divine presence in nature and the human soul, she found refuge in the life of the imagination, poems, letter writing, and caring for her dog Carlo.

By 1858, Dickinson had made clean copies of many of her earlier poems and began binding them in small, sewn sheaves. Over the course of the next seven years, she pieced together 40 bound manuscripts—not uncovered until after her death—that contained some 800 original poems. After undergoing an emotional disturbance of unknown origin, Dickinson withdrew from social interaction in the early 1860s, diagnosed by a physician as suffering "nervous prostration."

Whatever the cause, the crisis sparked her poetic imagination, and the five years from 1860 to 1865 were her most productive. Cloistered in an upstairs room at the family residence on North Pleasant Street, she wrote vigorous, rhapsodic lyrics and elegies in an idiosyncratic style that was misunderstood and unappreciated by contemporaries. Her poetry, which she called "my letter to the world," frequently referred to herself as a bee gathering nectar. In "The Poets light but Lamps" (ca. 1864), she implied that her immortality hinged on the survival of her verse.

By 1867, Dickinson spoke to outsiders only through the door and interacted primarily with nieces, nephews, and neighborhood children. Finding private joy in nature, she collected sweet peas and flowers for pressing in notebooks and proclaimed "Exhilaration is the Breeze" (1868). Other poems plumbed the depths of her inner life. "Tell all the Truth but tell it slant" (ca. 1868) captures the torments of social restraint; "I should not dare to be so sad" (1871) refers to the grief of losing family members and friends.

In 1872, eyestrain and nephritis complicated the burdens of baking for the family and nursing her mother through senility and paralytic stroke. As a result, the poet retreated even further, immersing herself in the writings of Charlotte and Emily Brontë, Elizabeth Barrett

A recently recovered daguerreotype of Emily Dickinson (*left*)—one of only two authenticated photos of the reclusive poet—shows her with friend Kate Scott Turner in 1859.

Browning, Lydia Maria Child, and George Eliot, longtime literary companions. Hinting at her own state of mind, she mourned, "So much of Heaven has gone from Earth" (ca. 1872).

Dickinson's style of versification violated literary standards of the day for punctuation, capitalization, and syntax. Clashes with newspaper and magazine editors over poems published in altered form ended her ventures into the critical market. Secluded in her private world, she continued to generate verse that defied categorization, such as the late laments "How lonesome the Wind must feel Nights" and "I have no Life but this" (both ca. 1877).

Upon the poet's death on May 15, 1886, her sister Lavinia disregarded Dickinson's request to burn 1,775 poems and 300 letters to sister-in-law Susan Huntington Gilbert Dickinson. *The Poems of Emily Dickinson,* a complete and mostly unaltered collection of her poetry, appeared in print for the first time in 1955 and soon established her reputation as America's greatest female poet.

Mary Ellen Snodgrass

Selected Poems, 1860–1863

The nearly 1,800 poems of Emily Dickinson, unorthodox and largely unknown in her lifetime, provide glimpses into the deep inner world of a reclusive but highly imaginative, skilled, and innovative verse maker. Many of her poems, like those presented below, date from the period 1860–1865 and address such themes as spiritual identity, the wonders of nature, and the creative imagination, as well as alienation, defiance, struggle, and death—all in delicate, hushed tones and a highly individual style. The numbers commonly used to designate Dickinson's poems, which carried no formal titles, are those assigned in Thomas H. Johnson's first complete collection of her verse, published in 1955.

(324), 1860

Some keep the Sabbath going to Church –
I keep it, staying at Home –
With a Bobolink for a Chorister –
And an Orchard, for a Dome –

Some keep the Sabbath in Surplice –
I just wear my Wings –
And instead of tolling the Bell, for Church,
Our little Sexton – sings.

God preaches, a noted Clergyman –
And the sermon is never long,
So instead of getting to Heaven, at least –
I'm going, all along.

(258), 1861

There's a certain Slant of light,
Winter Afternoons –
That oppresses, like the Heft
Of Cathedral Tunes –

Heavenly Hurt, it gives us –
We can find no scar,
But internal difference,
Where the Meanings, are –

None may teach it – Any –
'Tis the Seal Despair –
An imperial affliction
Sent us of the air –

When it comes, the Landscape listens –
Shadows – hold their breath –
When it goes, 'tis like the Distance
On the look of Death –

(465), 1862

I heard a Fly buzz – when I died –
The Stillness in the Room
Was like the Stillness in the Air –
Between the Heaves of Storm –

The Eyes around – had wrung them dry –
And Breaths were gathering firm
For that last Onset – when the King
Be witnessed – in the Room –

I willed my Keepsakes – Signed away
What portions of me be
Assignable – and then it was
There interposed a Fly –

With Blue – uncertain, stumbling Buzz –
Between the light – and me –
And then the Windows failed – and then
I could not see to see –

(712), 1863

Because I could not stop for Death –
He kindly stopped for me –
The Carriage held but just Ourselves –
And Immortality.

We slowly drove – He knew no haste
And I had put away
My labor and my leisure too,
For His Civility –

We passed the School, where Children strove
At Recess – in the Ring –
We passed the Fields of Gazing Grain –
We passed the Setting Sun –

Or rather – He passed us –
The Dews drew quivering and chill –
For only Gossamer, my Gown –
My Tippet – only Tulle –

We paused before a House that seemed
A Swelling of the Ground –
The Roof was scarcely visible –
The Cornice – in the Ground –

Since then – ’tis Centuries – and yet
Feels shorter than the Day
I first surmised the Horses’ Heads
Were toward Eternity –

Source: Bartleby.com (www.bartleby.com).

Douglass, Frederick

(ca. 1818–1895)

Slave, freedman, abolitionist, civil rights activist, orator, newspaper editor, and diplomat Frederick Douglass was, and arguably remains, the most famous and respected African American of the nineteenth century. Having escaped from slavery at the age of about 20, he became an eloquent champion of liberty and equality, eventually serving his country as a government official and adviser to presidents. His first autobiographical work, *Narrative of the Life of Frederick Douglass, an American Slave* (1845), was highly influential in advancing the abolitionist cause and came to be regarded as a masterpiece of the American literary renaissance. Two later autobiographies, *My Bondage and My Freedom* (1855) and *Life and Times of Frederick Douglass* (1881), expanded on the details of his early life, his escape from bondage, and his thoughts on slavery and race.

Slave Years

Sometime around 1818—he never knew for certain—Frederick Augustus Washington Bailey was born to a slave woman named Harriet Bailey on Maryland's Eastern Shore. He also never knew the identity of his father, though he suspected it was his white owner, Aaron Anthony. The boy had one older brother and four sisters. His mother was sold when Douglass was only weeks old, and he was raised by his maternal grandmother, Betsey Bailey, until the age of about 6.

In 1824, his grandmother brought him to a plantation in Talbot County, where Anthony was working as an overseer, and left him there. Two years, later, upon the death of his master, the boy became the property of Anthony's son-in-law, Thomas Auld, who sent Douglass to live with his brother, Hugh Auld, in Baltimore. Hugh's wife

Sophia began teaching Douglass to read, until Hugh found out about the lessons and warned her that it was both unlawful and unsafe to teach slaves to read. Douglass recognized this as a turning point in his life, later observing that education would be his "pathway from slavery to freedom." While forbidden to learn to read and write, the boy spent the next several years educating himself in secret; sometimes he would give his food to poor white boys in exchange for lessons.

After seven years in Baltimore, Douglass was sent in 1833 to live in St. Michaels, Maryland, where he returned to work for Thomas Auld. When Auld found Douglass teaching other slaves to read, he rented him out to a farmer named Edward Covey, hoping the renowned "slave breaker" would make Douglass more obedient. Covey beat Douglass nearly every day and almost succeeded in breaking him. One day, however, Douglass chose to fight back. The two men fought to a draw, but the incident reignited Douglass's will to live and desire for freedom. The fight, he wrote, "rekindled the few expiring embers of freedom, and revived within me a sense of my own manhood."

Covey finally gave up trying to break Douglass, instead sending him to work for William Freeland, another local farmer. There, the incorrigible teenage slave organized a Sunday school and, true to his belief that education was the key to freedom, again began teaching fellow slaves to read. A failed escape in 1836 landed him in jail and then back in Baltimore with Hugh and Sophia Auld, who hired him out to work as a caulker in a shipyard. Over the next two years, Douglass prepared for a second escape attempt.

Early Years as a Free Man

Enjoying greater mobility than he had as a plantation slave, Douglass joined the East Baltimore Mental Improvement Society in 1837 and met his future wife, Anna Murray. In fall 1838, dressed in a sailor's uniform and carrying identification papers borrowed from a free black man, Douglass finally escaped to New York, where he changed his last name to Johnson. Anna succeeded in following him out of Maryland, and the couple married less than two weeks later. They then moved to New Bedford, Massachusetts, where they changed their last name to Douglass to hide from slave catchers.

Frederick Douglass escaped slavery in Maryland at the age of about 20 (he was never sure of his exact age) and published his first, highly influential autobiography in 1845.

The years in New Bedford were good to the family. The couple had four children there—Rosetta (1839), Lewis Henry (1840), Frederick (1842), and Charles Remond (1844)—and Douglass gained prominence as an antislavery activist. (Daughter Annie was born in Rochester, New York, in 1849.) He attended abolitionist meetings, became a licensed preacher for the African Methodist Episcopal Zion Church, and subscribed to William Lloyd Garrison's abolitionist weekly *The Liberator.*

After hearing a fiery abolitionist oration by Garrison in 1841, Douglass was inspired to speak out about his own experiences as a slave. After one such speech, at the Massachusetts Anti-Slavery Society's annual convention in Nantucket, the group hired Douglass as a regular speaker. Over the next four years, traveling with Garrison, he became one of the most powerful and effective orators in the abolitionist movement. In 1845, responding to accusations that no ex-slave could be so articulate, Douglass told his story in the *Narrative,* which went into nine printings over the next three years. Though the book marked a turning point in Douglass's life, it was also a dangerous gamble.

Fearing recapture, Douglass heeded the advice of friends and embarked on a two-year tour of England, Scotland, and Ireland. While he traveled and lectured, English supporters raised more than $700 to purchase his freedom from the Auld family. Upon his return to the United States in the spring of 1847, Douglass was legally free.

Publisher and Activist

Douglass and his family moved to Rochester, New York, where he used money raised by his English friends to buy a printing press and publish his own abolitionist weekly paper. He called it *The North Star,* with a masthead that read, "Right is of no Sex—Truth is of no Color—God is the Father of us all, and we are all brethren."

True to that pronouncement, Douglass spent the remainder of the antebellum period fighting tirelessly for racial and gender equality and an end to slavery. Activities in the succeeding years included attendance at the first women's rights convention in Seneca Falls, New York, in 1848; concerted efforts on behalf of the Underground Railroad; and, after one of his daughters was forced to leave school because she was black, a fight to desegregate the Rochester public school system.

The move to Rochester also proved important for Douglass's intellectual independence. In 1851, he merged *The North Star* with Gerrit Smith's *Liberty Party Paper,* calling the new weekly *Frederick Douglass's Paper.* Not long thereafter, Douglass found himself at odds with his old friend Garrison, who believed that the federal government was too corrupt to bring an end to slavery and burned a copy of the U.S. Constitution to make his point. Douglass disagreed, arguing that change could be made within the existing political system. The rift between Garrison and Douglass mirrored the larger split between "radical" and "political" abolitionists.

The 1850s tested the optimism of Douglass and other black abolitionists. The political and social roller-coaster ride of the sectional crisis forced Douglass and others to hold tight to their faith in a brighter future as they struggled in the midst of overwhelming odds. The U.S. Supreme Court ruling in the case of *Dred Scott v. Sandford* (1857) struck a devastating blow to Douglass's efforts for racial equality—and his outlook—by declaring that blacks were "beings of an inferior order" and could never be U.S. citizens. During the summer of 1859, after abolitionist zealot John Brown launched a raid on the federal arsenal at Harpers Ferry, Virginia (now West Virginia), in hopes of inciting a mass slave rebellion, Douglass was forced to leave the country when it was discovered that he had visited Brown two months earlier. Although Douglass disapproved of Brown's plan, his philosophy had changed: He had come to believe that slavery could be abolished only through violence.

Returning safely to Rochester from Canada in April 1860, Douglass watched the nation devolve into civil war over the course of the next year—and welcomed the conflict as a new American Revolution. An advocate for change and voice of his people, he applied his full moral force and eloquence during the war years to urging President Lincoln and other Union leaders to focus on—and proclaim—emancipation as the highest objective of the war effort, while helping the African American community maintain hope and faith in the future. After the Emancipation Proclamation in 1863, Douglass urged the president to allow black men to fight for the Union. That spring, he recruited for the Fifty-fourth Massachusetts Volunteer Infantry, the nation's first regiment of black soldiers. His sons Lewis and Charles both served in the regiment.

With the end of the war and ratification of the Thirteenth Amendment, Douglass finally realized his dream of an end to slavery. He spent the remaining years of his life fighting for black equality, editing and writing, advising several Republican administrations, and serving as U.S. minister to Haiti from 1889 to 1891. He died of a heart attack on February 20, 1895, shortly after delivering a speech on women's rights.

A. Kristen Foster

See also: Abolitionist and Antislavery Movements; Garrison, William Lloyd; Slavery and Slave Life

Chapter One, *Narrative of the Life of Frederick Douglass, an American Slave,* 1845

The most celebrated and influential work in the genre of the slave narrative, Frederick Douglass's first autobiography (there would be two more) was at once a compelling personal memoir of his experiences in bondage, the evolution of his moral and intellectual identity, and his quest for physical freedom, as well as an eloquent treatise on slavery and abolitionism. Chapter One, which recounts his early life on Maryland's Eastern Shore, lacks some of the basic details of more conventional autobiographies, as he does not know the date, or even year, of his birth and can only suspect the identity of his father. The chapter concludes with an account of his first exposure to the kind of extreme brutality visited upon slaves by their masters—the whipping of his Aunt Hester—and its profound effect on him for the rest of his life.

I was born in Tuckahoe, near Hillsborough, and about twelve miles from Easton, in Talbot county, Maryland. I have no accurate knowledge of my age, never having seen any authentic record containing it. By far the larger part of the slaves know as little of their ages as horses know of theirs, and it is the wish of most masters within my knowledge to keep their slaves thus ignorant. I do not remember to have ever met a slave who could tell of his birthday. They seldom come nearer to it than planting-time, harvest-time, cherry-time, spring-time, or fall-time. A want of information concerning my own was a source of unhappiness to me even during childhood. The white children could tell their ages. I could not tell why I ought to be deprived of the same privilege. I was not allowed to make any inquiries of my master concerning it. He deemed all such inquiries on the part of a slave improper and impertinent, and evidence of a restless spirit. The nearest estimate I can give makes me now between twenty-seven and twenty-eight years of age. I come to this, from hearing my master say, some time during 1835, I was about seventeen years old.

My mother was named Harriet Bailey. She was the daughter of Isaac and Betsey Bailey, both colored, and quite dark. My mother was of a darker complexion than either my grandmother or grandfather.

My father was a white man. He was admitted to be such by all I ever heard speak of my parentage. The opinion was also whispered that my master was my father; but of the correctness of this opinion, I know nothing; the means of knowing was withheld from me. My mother and I were separated when I was but an infant—before I knew her as my mother. It is a common custom, in the part of Maryland from which I ran away, to part children from their mothers at a very early age. Frequently, before the child has reached its twelfth month, its mother is taken from it, and hired out on some farm a considerable distance off, and the child is placed under the care of an old woman, too old for field labor. For what this separation is done, I do not know, unless it be to hinder the development of the child's affection toward its mother, and to blunt and destroy the natural affection of the mother for the child. This is the inevitable result.

I never saw my mother, to know her as such, more than four or five times in my life; and each of these times was very short in duration, and at night. She was hired by a Mr. Stewart, who lived about twelve miles from my home. She made her journeys to see me in the night, travelling the whole distance on foot, after the performance of her day's work. She was a field hand, and a whipping is the penalty of not being in the field at sunrise, unless a slave has special permission from his or her master to the contrary—a permission which they seldom get, and one that gives to him that gives it the proud name of being a kind master. I do not recollect of ever seeing my mother by the light of day. She was with me in the night. She would lie down with me, and get me to sleep, but long before I waked she was gone. Very little communication ever took place between us. Death soon ended what little we could have while she lived, and with it her hardships and suffering. She died when I was about seven years old, on one of my master's farms, near Lee's Mill. I was not allowed to be present during her illness, at her death, or burial. She was gone long before I knew any thing about it. Never having enjoyed, to any considerable extent, her soothing presence, her tender and watchful care, I received the tidings of her death with much the same emotions I should have probably felt at the death of a stranger.

Called thus suddenly away, she left me without the slightest intimation of who my father was. The whisper that my master was my father, may or may not be true; and, true or false, it is of but little consequence to my purpose whilst the fact remains, in all its glaring odiousness, that slaveholders have ordained, and by law established, that the children of slave women shall in all cases follow the condition of their mothers; and this is done too obviously to administer to their own lusts, and make a gratification of their wicked desires profitable as well as pleasurable; for by this cunning arrangement, the slaveholder, in cases not a few, sustains to his slaves the double relation of master and father.

I know of such cases; and it is worthy of remark that such slaves invariably suffer greater hardships, and have more to contend with, than others. They are, in the first place, a constant offence to their mistress. She is ever disposed to find fault with them; they can seldom do any thing to please her; she is never better pleased than when she sees them under the lash, especially when she suspects her husband of showing to his mulatto children favors which he withholds from his black slaves. The master is frequently compelled to sell this class of his slaves, out of deference to the feelings of his white wife; and, cruel as the deed may strike any one to be, for a man to sell his own children to human flesh-mongers, it is often the dictate of humanity for him to do so; for, unless he does this, he must not only whip them himself, but must stand by and see one white son tie up his brother, of but few shades darker complexion than himself, and ply the gory lash to his naked back; and if he lisp one word of disapproval, it is set down to his parental partiality, and only makes a bad matter worse, both for himself and the slave whom he would protect and defend.

Every year brings with it multitudes of this class of slaves. It was doubtless in consequence of a knowledge of this fact, that one great statesman of the south predicted the downfall of slavery by the inevitable laws of population. Whether this prophecy is ever fulfilled or not, it is nevertheless plain that a very different-looking class of people are springing up at the south, and are now held in slavery, from those originally brought to this country from Africa; and if their increase do no other good, it will do away the force of the argument, that God cursed Ham, and therefore American slavery is right. If the lineal descendants of Ham are alone to be scripturally enslaved, it is certain that slavery at the south must soon become unscriptural; for thousands are ushered into the world, annually, who, like myself, owe their existence to white fathers, and those fathers most frequently their own masters.

The louder she screamed, the harder he whipped; and where the blood ran fastest, there he whipped longest.

I have had two masters. My first master's name was Anthony. I do not remember his first name. He was generally called Captain Anthony—a title which, I presume, he acquired by sailing a craft on the Chesapeake Bay. He was not considered a rich slaveholder. He owned two or three farms, and about thirty slaves. His farms and slaves were under the care of an overseer. The overseer's name was Plummer. Mr. Plummer was a miserable drunkard, a profane swearer, and a savage monster. He always went armed with a cowskin and a heavy cudgel. I have known him to cut and slash the women's heads so horribly, that even master would be enraged at his cruelty, and would threaten to whip him if he did not mind himself. Master, however, was not a humane slaveholder. It required extraordinary barbarity on the part of an overseer to affect him. He was a cruel man, hardened by a long life of slaveholding. He would at times seem to take great pleasure in whipping a slave. I have often been awakened at the dawn of day by the most heart-rending shrieks of an own aunt of mine, whom he used to tie up to a joist, and whip upon her naked back till she was literally covered with blood. No words, no tears, no prayers, from his gory victim, seemed to move his iron heart from its bloody purpose. The louder she screamed, the harder he whipped; and where the blood ran fastest, there he whipped longest. He would whip her to make her scream, and whip her to make her hush; and not until overcome by fatigue, would he cease to swing the blood-clotted cowskin. I remember the first time I ever witnessed this horrible exhibition. I was quite a child, but I well remember it. I never shall forget it whilst I remember any thing. It was the first of a long series of such outrages, of which I was doomed to be a witness and a participant. It struck me with awful force. It was the blood-stained gate, the entrance to the hell of slavery, through which I was about to pass. It was a most terrible spectacle. I wish I could commit to paper the feelings with which I beheld it.

This occurrence took place very soon after I went to live with my old master, and under the following circumstances. Aunt Hester went out one night,—where or for what I do not know,—and happened to be absent when my master desired her presence. He had ordered her not to go out evenings, and warned her that she must never let him catch her in company with a young man, who was paying attention to her belonging to Colonel Lloyd. The young man's name was Ned Roberts, generally called Lloyd's Ned. Why master was so careful of her, may be safely left to conjecture. She was a woman of noble form, and of graceful proportions, having very few equals, and fewer superiors, in personal appearance, among the colored or white women of our neighborhood.

Aunt Hester had not only disobeyed his orders in going out, but had been found in company with Lloyd's Ned; which circumstance, I found, from what he said while whipping her, was the chief offence. Had he been a man of pure morals himself, he might have been thought interested in protecting the innocence of my aunt; but those who knew him will not suspect him of any such virtue. Before he commenced whipping Aunt Hester, he took her into the kitchen, and stripped her from neck to waist, leaving her neck, shoulders, and back, entirely naked. He then told her to cross her hands, calling her at the same time a d——d b——h. After crossing her hands, he tied them with a strong rope, and led her to a stool under a large hook in the joist, put in for the purpose. He made her get upon the stool, and tied her hands to the hook. She now stood fair for his infernal purpose. Her arms were stretched up at their full length, so that she stood upon the ends of her toes. He then said to her, "Now, you d——d b——h, I'll learn you how to disobey my orders!" and after rolling up his sleeves, he commenced to lay on the heavy cowskin, and soon the warm, red blood (amid heart-rending shrieks from her, and horrid oaths from him) came dripping to the floor. I was so terrified and horror-stricken at the sight, that I hid myself in a closet, and dared not venture out till long after the bloody transaction was over. I expected it would be my turn next. It was all new to me. I had never seen any thing like it before. I had always lived with my grandmother on the outskirts of the plantation, where she was put to raise the children of the younger women. I had therefore been, until now, out of the way of the bloody scenes that often occurred on the plantation.

Source: Frederick Douglass, *Narrative of the Life of Frederick Douglass, an American Slave* (London: H.G. Collins, 1851).

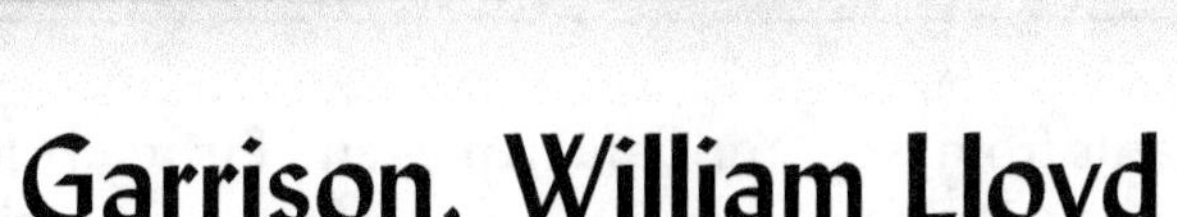

Garrison, William Lloyd

(1805–1879)

As a newspaper editor, writer, and orator, William Lloyd Garrison was the most visible and outspoken leader of the antislavery movement and the personification of its radical wing for more than three decades. He is best known as the founder and editor of the Boston-based antislavery weekly *The Liberator,* which played a vital role in communicating the views and principles of the movement from January 1831 through December 1865. During that span, Garrison was at the center of the movement that called for the immediate, unconditional emancipation of all slaves in the United States.

He was born in Newburyport, Massachusetts, on December 12, 1805. His father, Abijah Garrison, abandoned the family when William was a young child. Raised by his mother, Frances Lloyd Garrison, William apprenticed as a shoemaker, clerk, and carpenter. Although the entire family moved to Baltimore in 1815, Garrison returned to Newburyport the following year, finding work as an apprentice at a newspaper called the *Newburyport Herald.* In 1826, with his apprenticeship complete, Garrison purchased his own newspaper, the *Essex Courant,* renaming it the *Free Press.* Even though Garrison's first experience as an editor was short-lived—he sold the *Free Press* in 1827—it deepened his commitment to a career in journalism.

During a visit to Boston in March 1828, Garrison was converted to the antislavery cause by a Baltimore-based Quaker named Benjamin Lundy. Garrison soon joined Lundy in coediting an antislavery newspaper called *The Genius of Universal Emancipation.* After serving 49 days in a Baltimore jail in 1830 for libeling a merchant and slave trader, Garrison spent the next year forging important relationships with fellow abolitionists. Brothers Arthur and Lewis Tappan, wealthy silk merchants from New York, and James and Lucretia Mott, a married couple from Pennsylvania, all greatly influenced Garrison's later efforts as an abolitionist.

The Liberator

Garrison published the first issue of *The Liberator* on January 1, 1831, circulating 400 copies in Boston. Like many opponents of slavery, he had supported a campaign in the 1820s for African colonization—whereby the slaves would be freed and returned to Africa—but ultimately concluded that neither colonization nor gradual emancipation was a feasible or just solution. Now a vocal opponent of colonization and its chief advocacy group, the American Colonization Society, Garrison used *The Liberator* to advance the cause of complete, immediate abolition.

In his first editorial, Garrison argued that slaves and free African Americans deserved to be full citizens of the United States on the basic principle that "all men are created equal." Apologizing for his earlier support of "the popular but pernicious doctrine of gradual abolition," Garrison asked for the "pardon of my God, of my country, and of my brethren the poor slaves, for having uttered a sentiment so full of timidity, injustice and absurdity." On the subject of slavery, he promised readers, "I will be as harsh as truth, and as uncompromising as justice. . . . I am in earnest—I will not equivocate—I will not excuse—I will not retreat a single inch—AND I WILL BE HEARD."

In addition to immediate abolition, Garrison used *The Liberator* to champion full civil rights for African Americans, to condemn racial discrimination of any kind, and to report on free labor issues playing out in Northern factories. It did not take long for the paper to become a target of Southern politicians, newspaper editors, and slave owners. In August 1831, in fact, *The Liberator* was falsely blamed for a role in the slave rebellion led by Nat Turner in Southampton County, Virginia, that resulted in the deaths of 60 whites. Although there is no evidence that Turner had ever read the paper, or even that it had been available in Southampton County, angry whites drew a connection between the launch of *The Liberator* in January and Turner's bloody uprising eight months later. In an editorial that September, Garrison disavowed blame but warned of continuing "sorrows" resulting from the crime of racial op-

Radical abolitionist William Lloyd Garrison, memorialized by a bronze statue in Boston's Back Bay, drew the ire of moderate antislavery advocates as well as Southern whites.

pression. "We are horror-struck at the late tidings," he wrote, but "IMMEDIATE EMANCIPATION alone can save [the land] from the vengeance of Heaven!"

Quick to accuse Garrison of inciting further rebellion, Southern authorities responded aggressively. In the Georgetown section of Washington, D.C., free African Americans faced a $25 fine and 30 days in jail for picking up copies of *The Liberator* at the post office; if the offender were unable to pay the fine and jail fees, he or she could be sold into slavery for four months. In Columbia, South Carolina, a vigilance committee offered a reward of $1,500 for turning in anyone distributing the paper. Georgia took even more drastic action, offering a $5,000 reward for Garrison's arrest and transportation to the state for trial on sedition and libel charges; nothing came of the threats.

Garrison, meanwhile, focused all of his energies on the newspaper and the cause of abolition. Although *The Liberator* had only 50 white subscribers as of early 1832, the paper had a wide readership among free African Americans in the North. In addition, opposing Southern publications picked up stories from the weekly and republished them with angry editorial comments. In doing so, they inadvertently helped Garrison spread his message beyond the paper's direct readership.

New Directions

Garrison's efforts on behalf of the antislavery movement were hardly limited to *The Liberator.* On January 6, 1832, meeting at Boston's African Baptist Church, Garrison and 12 fellow abolitionists formed the New England Anti-Slavery Society; *The Liberator* served as its official organ. Also that year, with funding from Arthur Tappan, Garrison published his book *Thoughts on African Colonization,* in which he declared that colonization was "inadequate in design, injurious in its operation, and contrary to sound principle."

In December of the following year, Garrison and Tappan founded the American Anti-Slavery Society (AASS), which convened an assembly of 62 delegates in Philadelphia. The delegates chose Garrison to write the new society's Declaration of Sentiments, which pledged a commitment to nonviolence, opposition to colonization and racial prejudice, and support for immediate abolition. The AASS distributed more than 100,000 pieces of antislavery literature in 1834 and began its "great postal campaign" in 1835, mailing a million pamphlets to politicians, ministers, and newspaper editors across the South.

During the course of the 1830s, Garrison and his supporters broadened their critique of society to include issues of women's rights and religious Perfectionism (the belief that it is possible to become free of sin through Christian faith). African American abolitionists such as Frederick Douglass and Charles L. Remond, however, objected to anything that distracted attention from the cause of abolishing slavery. Although Garrison and Douglass had become close friends when the latter began lecturing in 1841, disagreements over how best to pursue abolition ultimately caused a rift between the two men. Douglass aggravated the situation in 1847 by starting his own newspaper, *The North Star,* and publicly broke with Garrison over support of the Free Soil Party as a means of ending slavery. Douglass preferred to work within the political system to fight the institution, while Garrison rejected the government as hopelessly corrupt. Harriet Beecher Stowe, author of the best-selling antislavery novel *Uncle Tom's Cabin* (1852), intervened in December 1853 and succeeded in calming the feud.

Abolition

As the sectional crisis deepened in the 1850s, Garrison stepped up his attacks on slavery. At a meeting of the Massachusetts Anti-Slavery Society on July 4, 1854, he burned a copy of the U.S. Constitution—calling it "a covenant with death, an agreement with hell"—to protest the recently passed Kansas-Nebraska Act. Although he maintained his commitment to pacifism, the outbreak of violence between proslavery and abolitionist forces in what became known as "Bleeding Kansas," followed by the disastrous raid on a federal arsenal at Harpers Ferry, Virginia (now West Virginia), led by radical abolitionist John Brown in 1859, soon made it clear to Garrison that violence would decide the future of slavery.

With the outbreak of the Civil War in April 1861, Garrison countered the view of President Abraham Lincoln and a majority of Northerners that the purpose of the conflict was to preserve the Union. In the May 3 issue of *The Liberator,* Garrison wrote that unless the war also brought an end to slavery, "there will be nothing to look for but heavier judgments and an irrevocable doom!"

In February 1865, after Congress passed the Thirteenth Amendment to the U.S. Constitution—which abolished slavery—Garrison proclaimed to readers, "Freedom is triumphant! THE PEOPLE have decreed the death of slavery!" Ratification of the amendment that December, the editor felt, marked an appropriate occasion to discontinue publication of *The Liberator.* His longtime mission "having been gloriously consummated," Garrison took leave of readers with the final issue on December 29, 1865. In his remaining years,

Garrison continued his campaign against racial prejudice and his support for such reform causes as woman suffrage and the prohibition of liquor. He died of kidney disease on May 24, 1879.

Justin Andrew Pariseau

See also: Abolitionist and Antislavery Movements; Douglass, Frederick

Final Editorial, *The Liberator,* December 29, 1865

With this farewell editorial in the last issue of his antislavery weekly, The Liberator*—the preeminent publication of the abolitionist movement from its inaugural issue in January 1831—William Lloyd Garrison expressed profound relief that, after decades of struggle, "the chains of the captive have been broken." With a "fresh baptism of the soul," however, Garrison ends the piece with a verse that exhorts readers to continue efforts in the cause of freedom.*

The last! the last! the last!
O, by that little word
How mny thoughts are stirred—
That sister of THE PAST!

The present number of *The Liberator* is the completion of its thirty-fifth volume, and the termination of its existence.

Commencing my editorial career when only twenty years of age, I have followed it continuously till I have attained my sixtieth year—first, in connection with *The Free Press,* in Newburyport, in the spring of 1826; next, with *The National Philanthropist,* in Boston, in 1827; next, with *The Journal of the Times,* in Bennington, Vt., in 1828—9; next, with *The Genius of Universal Emancipation*, in Baltimore, in 1829—30; and, finally, with the *Liberator,* in Boston, from the 1st of January, 1831, to the 1st of

January, 1866;—at the start, probably the youngest member of the editorial fraternity in the land, now, perhaps, the oldest, not in years, but in continuous service,—unless Mr. Bryant, of the New York *Evening Post,* be an exception.

Whether I shall again be connected with the press, in a similar capacity, is quite problematical; but, at my period of life, I feel no prompting to start a new journal at my own risk, and with the certainty of struggling against wind and tide, as I have done in the past.

I began the publication of the *Liberator* without a subscriber, and I end it—it gives me unalloyed satisfaction to say—without a farthing as the pecuniary result of the patronage extended to it during thirty-five years of unremitted labors.

From the immense change wrought in the national feeling and sentiment on the subject of slavery, the *Liberator* derived no advantage at any time in regard to its circulation. The original disturber of the peace, nothing was left undone at the beginning, and up to the hour of the late rebellion, by Southern slaveholding villany on the one hand, and Northern pro-slavery malice on the other, to represent it as too vile a sheet to be countenanced by any claiming to be Christian or patriotic; and it always required rare moral courage or singular personal independence to be among its patrons. Never had a journal to look such opposition in the face—never was one so constantly belied and caricatured. If it had advocated all the crimes forbidden by the moral law of God and the statutes of the State, instead of vindicating the sacred claims of oppressed and bleeding humanity, it could not have been more vehemently denounced or more indignantly repudiated. To this day—such is the force of prejudice—there are multitudes who cannot be induced to read a single number of it, even on the score of curiosity, though their views on the slavery question are now precisely those which it has uniformly advocated. Yet no journal has been conducted with such fairness and impartiality; none has granted such freedom in its columns to its opponents; none has so scrupulously and uniformly presented all sides of every question discussed in its pages; none has so readily and exhaustively published, without note or comment, what its enemies have said to its disparagement, and the vilification of its editor; none has vindicated primitive Christianity, in its spirit and purpose—the higher law, in its supremacy over nations and governments as well as individual conscience—the Golden Rule, in its binding obligation upon all classes—the Declaration of Independence, with its self-evident truths—the rights of human nature, without distinction of race, complexion or sex—more earnestly or more uncompromisingly; none has exerted a higher moral or more broadly reformatory influence upon those who have given it a careful perusal; and none has gone beyond it in asserting the Fatherhood of God and the brotherhood of man. All this may be claimed for it without egotism or presumption. It has ever been a terror to evil-doers, and a praise to them that do well. It has excited the fierce hostility of all that is vile and demoniacal in the land, and won the affection and regard of the purest and noblest of the age. To me it has been unspeakably cheering, and the richest compensation for whatever of peril, suffering and defamation I have been called to encounter, that one uniform testimony has been borne, by those who have had, its weekly perusal, as to the elevating and quickening influence of the *Liberator* upon their character and lives; and the deep grief they are expressing in view of its discontinuance is overwhelmingly affecting to my feelings. Many of these date their subscription from the commencement of the paper, and they have allowed nothing in its columns to pass without a rigid scrutiny. They speak, therefore, experimentally, and testify of that which they have seen and do know. Let them be assured that my regret in the separation which is to take place between us, in consequence of the discontinuance of the *Liberator,* is at least as poignant as their own; and let them feel, as I do, comforted by the thought that it relates only to the weekly method of communicating with each other, and not to the principles we have espoused in the past, or the hopes and aims we cherish as to the future.

Although the *Liberator* was designed to be, and has ever been, mainly devoted to the abolition of slavery, yet it has been instrumental in aiding the cause of reform in many of its most important aspects.

I have never consulted either the subscription list of the paper or public sentiment in printing, or omitting to print, any article touching any matter whatever. Personally, I have never asked any one to become a subscriber, nor any one to contribute to its support, nor presented its claims for a better circulation in any lecture or speech, or at any one of the multitudinous anti-slavery gatherings in the land. Had I done so, no doubt its subscription list might have been much enlarged.

In this connection, I must be permitted to express my surprise that I am gravely informed, in various quarters, that this is no time to retire from public labor; that though the chains of the captive have been broken, he is yet to be vindicated in regard to the full possession of equal civil and political rights; that the freedmen in every part of the South are subjected to many insults and outrages; that the old slaveholding spirit is showing itself in every available form; that there is imminent danger that, in the hurry of reconstruction and readmission to the Union, the late rebel States will be left free to work any amount of mischief; that there is manifestly a severe struggle yet to come with the Southern powers of darkness, which will require the utmost vigilance and the most determined efforts on the part of the friends of impartial liberty—&c., &c., &c. Surely, it is not meant by all this that I am therefore bound to continue the publication of the *Liberator;* for that is a matter for me to determine, and no one else. As I commenced its publication without asking leave of any one, so I claim to be competant to decide when it may fitly close its career.

Again—it cannot be meant, by this presentation of the existing state of things at the South, either to impeach my intelligence, or to impute to me a lack of interest in behalf of that race, for the liberation and elevation of which I have labored so many years. If, when they had no friends, and no hope of earthly redemption, I did not hesitate to make their cause my own, is it to be supposed that, with their yokes broken, and their friends and advocates multiplied indefinitely, I can be any the less disposed to stand by them to the last—to insist on the full measure of justice and equity being meted out of them—to retain in my breast a lively and permanent interest in all that relates to their present condition and future welfare?

I shall sound no trumpet and make no parade as to what I shall do for the future. After having gone through with such a struggle as has never been paralleled in duration in the life of any reformer, and for nearly forty years been the target at which all poisonous and deadly missiles have been hurled, and having seen our great national iniquity blotted out, and freedom proclaimed throughout all the land to all the inhabitants thereof, and a thousand presses and pulpits supporting the claims of the colored population to fair treatment where not one could be found to do this in the early days of the anti-slavery conflict, I might—it seems to me—be so. But, as yet, I have neither asked nor wished to be relieved of any burdens or labors connected with the good old cause. I see a mighty work of enlightenment and regeneration yet to be accomplished at the South, and many cruel wrongs done to the freedmen which are yet to be redressed; and I neither counsel others to turn away from the field of conflict, under the delusion that no more remains to be done, nor contemplate such a course in my own case.

The object for which the *Liberator* was commenced—the extermination of chattel slavery—having been gloriously consummated, it seems to me specially appropriate to let its existence cover the historic period of the great struggle; leaving what remains to be done to complete the work of emancipation to other instrumentalities, (of which I hope to avail myself,) under new auspices, with more abundant means, and with millions instead of hundreds for allies.

Most happy am I to be no longer in conflict with the mass of my fellow-countrymen on the subject of slavery. For no man of any refinement or sensibility can be indifferent to the approbation of his fellow men, if it be rightly earned. But to obtain it by going with the multitude to do evil—by pandering to despotic power or a corrupt public sentiment—is self-degradation and personal dishonor:

> For more true joy Marcellus exiled feels,
> Than Caesar with a senate at his heels.

Better to be always in a minority of one with God—branded as madman, incendiary, fanatic, heretic, infidel—frowned upon by the powers that be, and mobbed by the populace—or consigned ignominiously to the gallows, like him whose soul is marching on, though his body lies mouldering in the grave, or burnt to ashes at the stake like Wickliffe, or nailed to the cross like him who gave himself for the world,—in defence of the RIGHT, than like Herod, having the shouts of a multitude, crying, It is the voice of a god, and not of a man!

Farewell, tried and faithful patrons! Farewell, generous benefactors, without whose voluntary but essential pecuniary contributions the *Liberator* must have long since been discontinued! Farewell, noble men and women who have wrought so long and so successfully, under God, to break every yoke! Hail, ye ransomed millions! Hail, year of jubilee! With a grateful heart and a fresh baptism of the soul, my last invocation shall be—

Spirit of Freedom! on—
    Oh! pause not in thy flight
Till every clime is won
    To worship in thy light:
Speed on thy glorious way,
    And wake the sleeping lands!
Millions are watching for the ray,
    And lift to thee their hands.
Still Onward! be thy cry—
    Thy banner on the blast;
And, like a tempest, as thou rushest by,
    Despots shall shrink aghast.
On! till thy name is known
    Throughout the peopled earth;
On! till thou reign'st alone,
    Man's heritage by birth;
On! till from every vale, and where the mountains rise,
The beacon lights of Liberty shall kindle to the skies!

WM. LLOYD GARRISON

Gettysburg Address

A revered speech delivered by President Abraham Lincoln on November 19, 1863, the Gettysburg Address remains one of the nation's most profound encomiums to patriotism and self-sacrifice. At the dedication of the Soldiers' National Cemetery on 17 acres in Gettysburg, Pennsylvania, four and a half months after the decisive Battle of Gettysburg, the two-minute eulogy provided a brief but enduring comment on martyrdom and the principles of American democracy.

Lincoln had received the invitation to speak only 17 days before the event. On the morning of the dedication, the president, dressed in a black suit, white gauntlets, and top hat, accompanied by Secretary of State William H. Seward and Secretary of the Treasury Salmon P. Chase, rode in a mile-long procession through the streets of Gettysburg with 15,000 mourners, local citizens and dignitaries, four military bands, and the governors of Indiana, Maryland, New Jersey, New York, Ohio, and Pennsylvania. Along Baltimore Street, the president was somber as he viewed the bullet holes, rifle pits, and general destruction left by the fighting.

For the four-hour ceremony, President Lincoln sat on the dais in a rocking chair. Following music by Birgfeld's Band and the U.S. Marine Band and a prayer by the Reverend Thomas H. Stockton, chaplain of the U.S. Senate, came the speech of statesman Edward Everett, a respected Greek revivalist at Harvard University. At noon, Everett delivered a two-hour oration on the Athenian statesman Pericles and on classical commentary at military funerals.

Sometime after 2 p.m., Lincoln stood before the crowd, bowed his head, and then, in a high tenor voice recognizable for its twangy Kentucky dialect, delivered from memory his 10-sentence, 272-word eulogy, which he had written on White House stationery and revised until that very morning. Viewers recalled that his lips quivered as he swept his hand toward the concentric semicircles formed of raw graves. Applause was sparse. An Associated Press stenographer telegraphed the speech to newspaper offices.

On November 24, the Harrisburg *Patriot and Union* dismissed the oration as a "silly" attempt to impress voters before the 1864 election. The Eaton, Ohio, *Register* of November 30 noted the address's quieting effect on the audience, which had been standing for hours. George William Curtis, in a commentary for *Harper's Weekly*, admired the speech for being "felicitous" and "earnest." Everett, in a letter to Lincoln on the day after the dedication, admitted that he had been bested by a two-minute speech that summarized what Everett had taken 120 minutes to say.

Lincoln's rhetoric set a standard for the concise definition of liberty while capturing the precarious state of a nation warring over essential issues of slavery and states' rights. His now iconic opening phrase—"Four score and seven years ago"—introduced a scriptural tone on the sacred occasion of burying young men who died in war. In simple, gracious terms, the president honored the nearly 8,000 Union and Confederate soldiers killed in three days of horrific fighting at Gettysburg for what he characterized as "the last full measure of devotion." And in looking to the "unfinished work" that lay ahead, he invoked a recurring imagery of life cycles to contrast the soldiers' martyrdom with a "new birth of freedom."

The president's skill at parallelism—"of the people, by the people, for the people"—stressed the essence of a governing system empowered by the will of common citizens rather than by aristocracy or royalty. In closing with a prophecy that the republic "shall not perish from the earth," the text lifted the day's events to global significance by portraying the United States as both a work in progress and a beacon of freedom to other nations.

Mary Ellen Snodgrass

See also: Lincoln, Abraham

Gettysburg Address, 1863

President Abraham Lincoln delivered his historic Gettysburg Address on November 19, 1863, at dedication ceremonies for Soldiers' National Cemetery in Gettysburg, Pennsylvania, where up to 8,000 Union and Confederate troops had died in hellish fighting the previous July. "The world will little note nor long remember what we say here," Lincoln declared in characteristic humility but, it would turn out, gross historical error. His brief oration—only 272 words long (as he penned them) and two minutes in delivery—became one of the most celebrated in the English language. In 1917, historian Orton H. Carmichael astutely referred to the Gettysburg Address as "America's Psalm." In 1992, Garry Wills rightly suggested the following in his book Lincoln at Gettysburg: *"The power of words has rarely been given a more compelling demonstration."*

> Four score and seven years ago our fathers brought forth on this continent a new nation, conceived in liberty and dedicated to the proposition that all men are created equal. Now we are engaged in a great civil war, testing whether that nation or any nation so conceived and so dedicated can long endure. We are met on a great battlefield of that war. We have come to dedicate a portion of that field as a final resting place for those who here gave their lives that that nation might live. It is altogether fitting and proper that we should do this. But in a larger sense, we cannot dedicate, we cannot consecrate, we cannot hallow this ground. The brave men, living and dead who struggled here have consecrated it far above our poor power to add or detract. The world will little note nor long remember what we say here, but it can never forget what they did here. It is for us the living rather to be dedicated here to the unfinished work which they who fought here have thus far so nobly advanced. It is rather for us to be here dedicated to the great task remaining before us—that from these honored dead we take increased devotion to that cause for which they gave the last full measure of devotion—that we here highly resolve that these dead shall not have died in vain, that this

nation, under God, shall have a new birth of freedom, and that government of the people, by the people, for the people, shall not perish from the earth.

Source: Abraham Lincoln Papers at the Library of Congress, Manuscript Division.

Grant, Ulysses S.

(1822–1885)

As commanding general of Union forces during the Civil War and two-term president of the United States during Reconstruction, Ulysses S. Grant was one of the dominant figures in mid-nineteenth-century American history. He is esteemed in literary circles for his two-volume autobiography, the *Personal Memoirs of Ulysses S. Grant* (1885), which publisher Mark Twain called "the best of any general's since Caesar."

Born Hiram Ulysses Grant on April 27, 1822, to tanner Jesse Root Grant and Hannah Simpson Grant in Point Pleasant, Ohio, he grew up on a farm in Brown County along the Ohio River. Despite being an unexceptional student, he won nomination at age 17 to the U.S. Military at West Point from his congressman, who incorrectly transcribed his name on the appointment papers as Ulysses Simpson Grant. He decided not to correct it but became known around the Academy as "Sam."

Military Career

Grant graduated from West Point in 1843, ranking in the middle of his class, and served with distinction under Generals Zachary Taylor and Winfield Scott in the Mexican-American War (1846–1848). Fighting in Mexico, he earned respect for his expert horsemanship and for two acts of bravery under fire, including the rescue of a fallen comrade.

Assigned to garrison duty after the war, Grant married Julia Boggs Dent, the sister of a West Point classmate, on August 22, 1848; she would become the mother of their daughter and three sons. Transferred to Washington Territory in 1853 and then to Fort Humboldt, California, he served on the West Coast for two years without Julia because his pay could not support a family. At age 32, Grant resigned his commission and returned to civilian life in St. Louis, Missouri. He sold real estate, collected customs duties, worked as county engineer, and then sold harnesses and saddles with his younger brothers, Orvil and Simpson, at a leather shop in Galena, Illinois.

With the outbreak of the Civil War in April 1861, Grant volunteered his services to the state militia; in May, the governor appointed him colonel of the 21st Illinois Volunteer Infantry. Grant proved highly successful in converting rowdy and inexperienced farm boys into soldiers, and President Abraham Lincoln named him brigadier general of volunteers in the Union army. Despite a less-than-stellar debut in combat command at the Battle of Belmont, in Missouri, in early November, Grant redeemed himself in Tennessee in February 1862, when his troops captured two strategic Southern forts—Henry and Donelson—that commanded the Tennessee and Cumberland Rivers and protected Nashville. These were the first major Union victories of the war, opening the state to Northern forces and raising hopes for a quick end to the conflict. For refusing to accept terms of capitulation from his Confederate counterpart at Fort Donelson, the Union commander earned a nickname by which he became nationally known: Unconditional Surrender Grant.

In early April 1862, Grant led Union forces in the bloody but indecisive Battle of Shiloh, which produced nearly 24,000 casualties between the two sides. That fall, he laid the Union siege at Vicksburg, Mississippi, that precipitated the Confederate surrender on July 4, 1863, effectively cutting off the trans-Mississippi states from the rest of the Confederacy. The fall of Vicksburg coincided with the Battle of Gettysburg in Pennsylvania, giving Union forces the momentum and strategic advantage to win the war. That November, in another key victory, Grant's forces rescued Union troops from a virtual siege at the hands of Confederate forces in the Battle of Chattanooga, reversed the campaign, and seized the offensive.

In gratitude for his fighting spirit and strategic successes, President Lincoln brought Grant to Washington, D.C., and appointed him general-in-chief of the Union army on March 12, 1864. In that capacity, Grant commanded the Army of the Potomac in Virginia from the Battle of the Wilderness (May 1864) through the Battle of Petersburg (June 1864 to March 1865). At the same time, he devised and directed what the Union had lacked—a concerted plan of action for total war on five fronts. His plan came to fruition with the final evacuation of the Confederate capital at Richmond on April 2, leading to the surrender of Southern forces by General Robert E. Lee at Appomattox Court House on April 9. Under the terms offered by Grant, Confederate troops were free to return home on their own mounts on the condition that they lay down their arms.

Union exultation over the victory proved short-lived. Less than two weeks later, on April 19, Grant served as a pallbearer at the funeral of President Lincoln.

Presidency

In 1868, still lionized for his Civil War heroics, Grant won the Republican nomination for president without opposition and ran in the general election against Democrat Horatio Seymour on a platform of national peace and amnesty for secessionists. Winning the November election handily, Grant entered the White House on March 4, 1869, as the youngest president of the United States to date, age 47. He immediately backed greenbacks with gold, modernized the national treasury, and secured monetary plates at the Bureau of Printing and Engraving to halt counterfeiting. By improving tax collection and boosting foreign trade, he lowered the national debt by $50 million.

With the former Confederate states under U.S. military command since passage of the Reconstruction Acts in 1867–1868, restoring the Union and integrating free blacks into society with full rights and citizenship remained high priorities of the Grant administration throughout his two terms. As president, he sided with Radical Republicans in Congress in implementing harsh policies against the former Confederate states and in support of black enfranchisement. An epidemic of vigilante violence against Southern blacks in the early 1870s gave rise to one of the most notable pieces of legislation Grant would sign, the Ku Klux Klan Act of 1871, which authorized the president to send in federal troops. The new Department of Justice, established the previous June, went on to issue 4,000 indictments and convict 1,150 Klan terrorists.

Other landmarks of Grant's first term include completion of the Transcontinental Railroad on May 10, 1869, which the president believed would help settle the frontier and facilitate commerce; establishment of the Yellowstone region of northwest Wyoming as the nation's first national park on March 1, 1872; and passage of the Amnesty Act of 1872, which restored citizenship to all but 500 secessionists.

Grant's policies toward Native Americans represented an effort to reverse the campaign of forced removal under way since the Andrew Jackson administration and to minimize military confrontation, albeit for the chief purpose of facilitating white settlement. Grant's Peace Policy included a reorganization of the Office of Indian Affairs and the mobilization of government agencies and Christian schools to ready Native Americans for citizenship. He appointed General Ely Samuel Parker, a native Seneca, as commissioner of Indian affairs and called for an emphasis on education, civilization, and protection. The number of Indian battles indeed fell dramatically during Grant's presidency, though the slaughter of buffalo herds—the main source of sustenance for Plains natives—continued unchecked.

Grant's hard-money policy during his first term won favor with the business and banking communities, though in 1869 he succeeded in foiling attempts by Jay Gould and James Fisk to corner the gold market. The president's popularity with the general electorate, combined with the support of the financial community and party bosses, swept him to a landslide victory in his 1872 reelection bid against liberal Republican candidate Horace Greeley, gadfly editor of the *New York Tribune.*

Grant's second term—indeed his entire presidency—fell under a cloud of scandal and corruption, combined with an economic crisis and strife over the late stages of Reconstruction. Although he initiated sweeping civil service reform to limit insider appointments and never faced accusations of direct involvement, close advisers to the president and other high-level members of the administration left office amid charges of graft, extortion, and profiteering. Among those implicated were the secretary of the treasury and his assistant, the secretary of the interior, the secretary of war, Grant's brother Orvil, and the president's private secretary, Orville Babcock. As Grant reeled under the scandals and reshuffled his cabinet, the country suffered

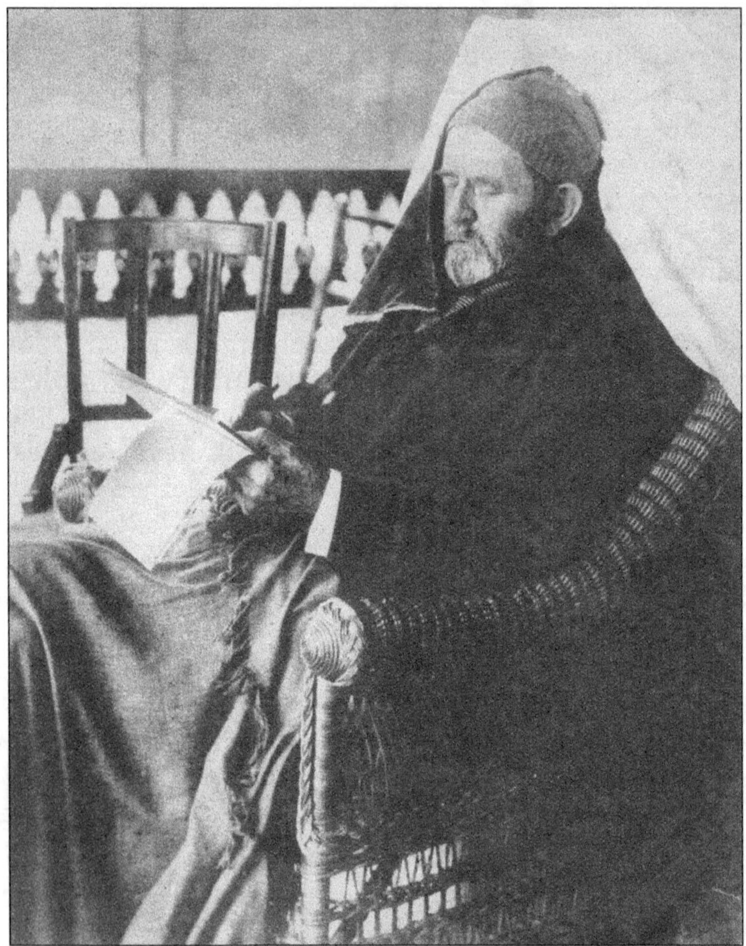

Former Civil War general and president Ulysses S. Grant worked on his two-volume *Personal Memoirs* from his sickbed and completed the work just days before dying.

the effects of the Panic of 1873, an economic depression that lasted five years and included a chain reaction of bank failures, railroad bankruptcies, business closures, and widespread unemployment.

His administration tainted, the economy in a shambles, and Reconstruction policy failing in key respects, Grant nevertheless harbored a desire for a third term. The Republican Party refused to break with the two-term tradition, however, and opted for Ohio governor Rutherford B. Hayes at the national convention of 1876. The deadlock between

Hayes and Democratic candidate Samuel Tilden in the general election ultimately resulted in the Compromise of 1877, by which Hayes became president but federal troops were withdrawn from the former Confederate states, bringing Reconstruction to an end.

Later Years

After leaving office in March 1877, Grant embarked with his wife and son on a two-year world tour, on which he was cheered by the public as a Civil War hero and welcomed by foreign leaders as a former president. He returned to America with aspirations for an unprecedented third term as president and had the support of the Stalwart faction of the Republican Party in 1880. Although he led after the first ballot at the party convention in Chicago, Grant finally lost to U.S. Representative James A. Garfield of Ohio on the thirty-sixth ballot.

His career in politics over, Grant moved to New York City, where he went into bankruptcy when his son's brokerage partner swindled and collapsed the firm in a Ponzi scheme. Diagnosed with throat and mouth cancer in 1884, perhaps due his longtime habit of smoking cigars, the former general and president focused his dwindling energy on resolving the family's financial situation. In a deal arranged by friend Mark Twain, Grant wrote for *The Century Magazine,* which paid him $500 each for three articles on the Battles of Shiloh and Vicksburg. The articles boosted magazine circulation by 100,000 and later served Stephen Crane as source material for his Civil War novel *The Red Badge of Courage* (1895).

The success of the articles led Grant to begin writing his memoirs, focusing primarily on his exploits in the Civil War. Writing from his sickroom at Mount McGregor near Saratoga, New York, Grant finished the work just days before his death, on July 23, 1885. Later that year, Twain's publishing company issued the *Personal Memoirs of Ulysses S. Grant* in two volumes. The firm sold a total of 350,000 sets, each containing the facsimile of a personal letter from Grant, generating an unprecedented $450,000 in royalties for his widow.

Mary Ellen Snodgrass

See also: Lincoln, Abraham; Reconstruction

◇◇

Chapter 67, *Personal Memoirs of Ulysses S. Grant,* 1885

◇◇

Finished just days before his death from throat cancer on July 23, 1885, the Personal Memoirs of Ulysses S. Grant *is the acclaimed work of a war hero and president who had little formal education and had not been known for his intellectual powers or literary abilities. Beginning with the words "Man proposes and God disposes" (Preface), the two-volume autobiography proceeds to a detailed account of his life—and a vivid, concise record of historical events—through the end of the Civil War. The subtitle to Chapter 67 summarizes the historic proceedings that brought the war to an end, as recounted by Grant: "Negotiations at Appomattox—Interview with Lee at McLean's House—The Terms of Surrender—Lee's Surrender—Interview with Lee after the Surrender." The full text of the chapter follows below.*

> On the 8th I had followed the Army of the Potomac in rear of Lee. I was suffering very severely with a sick headache, and stopped at a farmhouse on the road some distance in rear of the main body of the army. I spent the night in bathing my feet in hot water and mustard, and putting mustard plasters on my wrists and the back part of my neck, hoping to be cured by morning. During the night I received Lee's answer to my letter of the 8th, inviting an interview between the lines on the following morning. But it was for a different purpose from that of surrendering his army, and I answered him as follows:
>
> > *HEADQUARTERS ARMIES OF THE U. S.,*
> > *April 9, 1865.*
> >
> > *GENERAL R. E. LEE,*
> > *Commanding C. S. A.*
> >
> > *Your note of yesterday is received. As I have no authority to treat on the subject of peace, the meeting proposed for ten a.m. to-day could lead to no good. I will state,*

however, General, that I am equally anxious for peace with yourself, and the whole North entertains the same feeling. The terms upon which peace can be had are well understood. By the South laying down their arms they will hasten that most desirable event, save thousands of human lives and hundreds of millions of property not yet destroyed. Sincerely hoping that all our difficulties may be settled without the loss of another life, I subscribe myself, etc.,

U. S. GRANT,
Lieutenant-General.

I proceeded at an early hour in the morning, still suffering with the headache, to get to the head of the column. I was not more than two or three miles from Appomattox Court House at the time, but to go direct I would have to pass through Lee's army, or a portion of it. I had therefore to move south in order to get upon a road coming up from another direction.

When the white flag was put out by Lee, as already described, I was in this way moving towards Appomattox Court House, and consequently could not be communicated with immediately, and be informed of what Lee had done. Lee, therefore, sent a flag to the rear to advise Meade and one to the front to Sheridan, saying that he had sent a message to me for the purpose of having a meeting to consult about the surrender of his army, and asked for a suspension of hostilities until I could be communicated with. As they had heard nothing of this until the fighting had got to be severe and all going against Lee, both of these commanders hesitated very considerably about suspending hostilities at all. They were afraid it was not in good faith, and we had the Army of Northern Virginia where it could not escape except by some deception. They, however, finally consented to a suspension of hostilities for two hours to give an opportunity of communicating with me in that time, if possible. It was found that, from the route I had taken, they would probably not be able to communicate with me and get an answer back within the time fixed unless the messenger should pass through the rebel lines.

Lee, therefore, sent an escort with the officer bearing this message through his lines to me.

April 9, 1865.

GENERAL: I received your note of this morning on the picket-line whither I had come to meet you and ascertain definitely what terms were embraced in your proposal of yesterday with reference to the surrender of this army. I now request an interview in accordance with the offer contained in your letter of yesterday for that purpose.

R. E. LEE, General.
LIEUTENANT-GENERAL U. S. GRANT
Commanding U. S. Armies.

When the officer reached me I was still suffering with the sick headache, but the instant I saw the contents of the note I was cured. I wrote the following note in reply and hastened on:

April 9, 1865.
GENERAL R. E. LEE,
Commanding C. S. Armies.

Your note of this date is but this moment (11.50 a.m.) received, in consequence of my having passed from the Richmond and Lynchburg road to the Farmville and Lynchburg road. I am at this writing about four miles west of Walker's Church and will push forward to the front for the purpose of meeting you. Notice sent to me on this road where you wish the interview to take place will meet me.

U. S. GRANT,
Lieutenant-General.

I was conducted at once to where Sheridan was located with his troops drawn up in line of battle facing the Confederate army near by. They were very much excited, and expressed their view that this was all a ruse employed to enable the Confederates to get away. They said they believed that Johnston was marching up from North Carolina now, and Lee was moving to join him; and they would whip the rebels where they now were in five minutes if I would only let them go in. But I had no doubt about the good faith of Lee, and pretty soon was conducted to where he was. I found him at the house of a Mr. McLean, at Appomattox Court House, with Colonel Marshall, one of his staff officers, awaiting my arrival. The head of his column was occupying a hill, on a portion of which was an apple orchard, beyond a little valley which separated it from that on the crest of which Sheridan's forces were drawn up in line of battle to the south.

Before stating what took place between General Lee and myself, I will give all there is of the story of the famous apple tree.

Wars produce many stories of fiction, some of which are told until they are believed to be true. The war of the rebellion was no exception to this rule, and the story of the apple tree is one of those fictions based on a slight foundation of fact. As I have said, there was an apple orchard on the side of the hill occupied by the Confederate forces. Running diagonally up the hill was a wagon road, which, at one point, ran very near one of the trees, so that the wheels of vehicles had, on that side, cut off the roots of this tree, leaving a little embankment. General Babcock, of my staff, reported to me that when he first met General Lee he was sitting upon this embankment with his feet in the road below and his back resting against the tree. The story had no other foundation than that. Like many other stories, it would be very good if it was only true.

I had known General Lee in the old army, and had served with him in the Mexican War; but did not suppose, owing to the difference in our age and rank, that he would remember me, while I would more naturally remember him distinctly, because he was the chief of staff of General Scott in the Mexican War.

When I had left camp that morning I had not expected so soon the result that was then taking place, and consequently was in rough garb. I was without a sword, as I usually was when on horseback on the field, and wore a soldier's blouse for a coat, with the shoulder straps of my rank to indicate to the army who I was. When I went into the house I found General Lee. We greeted each other, and after shaking hands took our seats. I had my staff with me, a good portion of whom were in the room during the whole of the interview.

What General Lee's feelings were I do not know. As he was a man of much dignity, with an impassible face, it was impossible to say whether he felt inwardly glad that the end had finally come, or felt sad over the result, and was too manly to show it. Whatever his feelings, they were entirely concealed from my observation; but my own feelings, which had been quite jubilant on the receipt of his letter, were sad and depressed. I felt like anything rather than rejoicing at the downfall of a foe who had fought so long and valiantly, and had suffered so much for a cause, though that cause was, I believe, one of the worst for which a people ever fought, and one for which there was the least excuse. I do not question, however, the sincerity of the great mass of those who were opposed to us.

General Lee was dressed in a full uniform which was entirely new, and was wearing a sword of considerable value, very likely the sword which had been presented by the State of Virginia; at all events, it was an entirely different sword from the one that would ordinarily be worn in the field. In my rough traveling suit, the uniform of a private with the straps of a lieutenant-general, I must have contrasted very strangely with a man so handsomely dressed, six feet high and of faultless form. But this was not a matter that I thought of until afterwards.

We soon fell into a conversation about old army times. He remarked that he remembered me very well in the old army; and I told him that as a matter of course I remembered him perfectly, but from the difference in our rank and years (there being about sixteen years' difference in our ages), I had thought it very likely that I had not attracted his attention sufficiently to be remembered by him after such a long interval. Our conversation grew so pleasant that I almost forgot the object of our meeting. After the conversation had run on in this style for some time, General Lee called my attention to the object of our meeting, and said that he had asked for this interview for the purpose of getting from me the terms I proposed to give his army. I said that I meant merely that his army should lay down their arms, not to take them up again during the continuance of the war unless duly and properly exchanged. He said that he had so understood my letter.

Then we gradually fell off again into conversation about matters foreign to the subject which had brought us together. This continued for some little time, when General Lee again interrupted the course of the conversation by suggesting that the terms I proposed to give his army ought to be written out. I called to General Parker, secretary on my staff, for writing materials, and commenced writing out the following terms:

APPOMATTOX C. H., VA.,
Ap 19th, 1865.

GEN. R. E. LEE,
Comd'g C. S. A.

GEN: In accordance with the substance of my letter to you of the 8th inst., I propose to receive the surrender of the Army of N. Va. on the following terms, to wit: Rolls of all the officers and men to be made in duplicate. One copy to be given to an officer designated by me, the other to be retained by such officer or officers as you may designate. The officers to give their individual paroles not to take up arms against the Government of the United States until properly exchanged, and each company or regimental commander sign a like parole for the men of their commands. The arms, artillery and public property to be parked and stacked, and turned over to the officer appointed by me to receive them. This will not embrace the side-arms of the officers, nor their private horses or baggage. This done, each officer and man will be allowed to return to their homes, not to be disturbed by United States authority so long as they observe their paroles and the laws in force where they may reside.

Very respectfully,

U. S. GRANT,
Lt. Gen.

When I put my pen to the paper I did not know the first word that I should make use of in writing the terms. I only knew what was in my mind, and I wished to express it clearly, so that there could be no mistaking it. As I wrote on, the thought occurred to me that the officers had their own private horses and effects, which were important to them, but of no value to us; also that it would be an unnecessary humiliation to call upon them to deliver their side arms.

No conversation, not one word, passed between General Lee and myself, either about private property, side arms, or kindred subjects. He appeared to have no objections to the terms first proposed; or if he had a point to make against them he wished to wait until they were in writing to make it. When he read over that part of the terms about side arms, horses and private property of the officers, he remarked, with some feeling, I thought, that this would have a happy effect upon his army.

Then, after a little further conversation, General Lee remarked to me again that their army was organized a little differently from the army of the United States (still maintaining by implication that we were two countries); that in their army the cavalrymen and artillerists owned their own horses; and he asked if he was to understand that the men who so owned their horses were to be permitted to retain them. I told him that as the terms were written they would not; that only the officers were permitted to take their private property. He then, after reading over the terms a second time, remarked that that was clear.

I then said to him that I thought this would be about the last battle of the war—I sincerely hoped so; and I said further I took it that most of the men in the ranks were small farmers. The whole country had been so raided by the two armies that it was doubtful whether they would be able to put in a crop to carry themselves and their families through the next winter without the aid of the horses they were then riding. The United States did not want them and I would, therefore, instruct the officers I left behind to receive the paroles of his troops to let every man of the Confederate army who claimed to own a horse or mule take the animal to his home. Lee remarked again that this would have a happy effect.

He then sat down and wrote out the following letter:

> *HEADQUARTERS ARMY OF NORTHERN VIRGINIA, April 9, 1865.*
>
> *GENERAL:—I received your letter of this date containing the terms of the surrender of the Army of Northern Virginia as proposed by you. As they are substantially the same as those expressed in your letter of the 8th inst., they are accepted. I will proceed to designate the proper officers to carry the stipulations into effect.*
>
> *R. E. LEE, General.*

While duplicates of the two letters were being made, the Union generals present were severally presented to General Lee.

The much talked of surrendering of Lee's sword and my handing it back, this and much more that has been said about it is the purest romance. The word sword or side arms was not mentioned by either of us until I wrote it in the terms. There was no premeditation, and it did not occur to me until the moment I wrote it down. If I had happened to omit it, and General Lee had called my attention to it, I should have put it in the terms precisely as I acceded to the provision about the soldiers retaining their horses.

General Lee, after all was completed and before taking his leave, remarked that his army was in a very bad condition for want of food, and that they were without forage; that his men had been living for some days on parched corn exclusively, and that he would have to ask me for rations and forage. I told him "certainly," and asked for how many men he wanted rations. His answer was "about twenty-five thousand;" and I authorized him to send his own commissary and quartermaster to Appomattox Station, two or three miles away, where he could have, out of the trains we had stopped, all the provisions wanted. As for forage, we had ourselves depended almost entirely upon the country for that.

Generals Gibbon, Griffin and Merritt were designated by me to carry into effect the paroling of Lee's troops before they should start for their homes—General Lee leaving Generals Longstreet, Gordon and Pendleton for them to confer with in order to facilitate this work. Lee and I then separated as cordially as we had met, he returning to his own lines, and all went into bivouac for the night at Appomattox.

Soon after Lee's departure I telegraphed to Washington as follows:

> *HEADQUARTERS APPOMATTOX C. H., VA.,*
> *April 9th, 1865, 4.30 p.m.*
>
> *HON. E. M. STANTON, Secretary of War,*
> *Washington.*
>
> *General Lee surrendered the Army of Northern Virginia this afternoon on terms proposed by myself. The accompanying additional correspondence will show the conditions fully.*
>
> *U. S. GRANT,*
> *Lieut.-General.*

When news of the surrender first reached our lines our men commenced firing a salute of a hundred guns in honor of the victory. I at once sent word, however, to have it stopped. The

Confederates were now our prisoners, and we did not want to exult over their downfall.

I determined to return to Washington at once, with a view to putting a stop to the purchase of supplies, and what I now deemed other useless outlay of money. Before leaving, however, I thought I would like to see General Lee again; so next morning I rode out beyond our lines towards his headquarters, preceded by a bugler and a staff-officer carrying a white flag.

Lee soon mounted his horse, seeing who it was, and met me. We had there between the lines, sitting on horseback, a very pleasant conversation of over half an hour, in the course of which Lee said to me that the South was a big country and that we might have to march over it three or four times before the war entirely ended, but that we would now be able to do it as they could no longer resist us. He expressed it as his earnest hope, however, that we would not be called upon to cause more loss and sacrifice of life; but he could not foretell the result. I then suggested to General Lee that there was not a man in the Confederacy whose influence with the soldiery and the whole people was as great as his, and that if he would now advise the surrender of all the armies I had no doubt his advice would be followed with alacrity. But Lee said, that he could not do that without consulting the President first. I knew there was no use to urge him to do anything against his ideas of what was right.

I was accompanied by my staff and other officers, some of whom seemed to have a great desire to go inside the Confederate lines. They finally asked permission of Lee to do so for the purpose of seeing some of their old army friends, and the permission was granted. They went over, had a very pleasant time with their old friends, and brought some of them back with them when they returned.

When Lee and I separated he went back to his lines and I returned to the house of Mr. McLean. Here the officers of both armies came in great numbers, and seemed to enjoy the meeting as much as though they had been friends separated for a long time while fighting battles under the same flag. For the time being it looked very much as if all thought of the war had escaped their minds. After an hour pleasantly passed in this way I set out on horseback, accompanied by my staff and a small escort, for Burkesville Junction, up to which point the railroad had by this time been repaired.

Sources: Bartleby.com (www.bartleby.com); Grant, Ulysses S. *Personal Memoirs* (New York: C.L. Webster, 1885).

Harper, Frances Ellen Watkins

(1825–1911)

Abolitionist, suffragist, poet, and author Frances Ellen Watkins Harper, known as "The Bronze Muse," became America's first successful black female journalist and the most popular black poet of her time. With four published novels in addition to several volumes of poetry, Harper was one of the most prolific and widely read African American writers of the nineteenth century. As a traveling speaker, she inspired audiences with readings from her poetry on abolition and, during Reconstruction, the rights of freed slaves.

Frances Ellen Watkins was born to free blacks in Baltimore, Maryland, on September 24, 1825. After the death of her parents in 1828, she was raised by her uncle and aunt, educator and civil rights activist William Watkins and his wife, Henrietta. At the Academy for Negro Youth, founded by her uncle under the auspices of the African Methodist Episcopal Church, Watkins studied rhetoric, elocution, composition, and the Bible. She loved to read and write and began composing poetry as a young girl.

At age 13, Watkins left school to work as a domestic and nanny for a Quaker family that operated a bookstore in downtown Baltimore. The family gave her access to books and encouraged her reading and writing. She published her first poems as a teenager in African American periodicals, including *Frederick Douglass's Paper.* Her first collection of verse, *Forest Leaves,* appeared in 1845 when she was just 20 years old; no copies survive.

In 1851, Watkins left Baltimore to accept a job teaching needlework at Union Seminary in Wilberforce, Ohio, where she was the first female faculty member. Two years later, unable to return to Maryland because of laws barring the entry of free blacks into the state, she moved to Philadelphia, joined the American Anti-Slavery

Society, and maintained a safehouse for fugitive slaves on the Underground Railroad, while continuing to work on her poetry and essays. From 1854 to 1860, she traveled throughout the East and Midwest as a lecturer on abolition, education for freedmen, and female equality.

At age 29, meanwhile, Watkins had published *Poems on Miscellaneous Subjects* (1854), a brisk seller that raised funds at abolitionist fairs. The collection included poems on slavery, women's rights, temperance, and Christianity. In 1858, in the *Anti-Slavery Bugle,* she issued "Bury Me in a Free Land," which would prove extremely popular in her readings on the abolitionist lecture circuit. Watkins also began serving as editor of the *Anglo-African Magazine,* which in 1859 published her short story "The Two Offers," in which the feminist protagonist tries to convince her cousin to reject two offers of marriage. The appearance of the story made Watkins the first African American author to publish a piece of short fiction.

Her activism slowed after marriage in 1860 to Fenton Harper, a widower with three children, and the birth of their daughter, Mary, in 1862. Now Frances Ellen Watkins Harper, she lived on a farm outside Columbus, Ohio, until the death of her husband in May 1864, whereupon she sold the property, moved with the children back East, and resumed her writing and lecturing career.

Fearing that Northern activists had lost interest in former slaves after the Civil War, Harper traveled around the South lecturing on racial unity and teaching practical skills, including reading and writing, to freed men and women. She combined her concern for the plight of freed slaves with efforts on behalf of black women in particular and women's rights in general. On May 10, 1866, she shared the platform with Susan B. Anthony and Elizabeth Cady Stanton at the National Woman's Rights Convention in New York City, where she delivered an impassioned and historic address on equal rights. "Justice is not fulfilled so long as woman is unequal before the law," Harper declared. "We are all bound up together in one great bundle of humanity, and society cannot trample on the weakest and feeblest of its members without receiving the curse in its own soul."

In 1867, she traveled the lecture circuit to Demopolis, Eufaula, Mobile, and Montgomery, Alabama; Darlington and Sumter, South Carolina; and Athens, Columbiana, and Greenville, Georgia, to deliver speeches on education, challenges to black voters, and white male aggression against black women. For the *Christian Recorder,* the journal of the African Methodist Episcopal Church, she serialized three novels, *Minnie's Sacrifice* (1869), *Sowing and Reaping* (1876–1877), and *Trial and Triumph* (1888–1889), studies of marriage and temperance reissued by feminists in the late twentieth century. One of her longest works, *Moses: A Story of the Nile* (1869), is a verse rendition of the biblical slave narrative.

Harper's dedication to equality and literacy remained unwavering into her later years. On the theme of Reconstruction, *Sketches in Southern Life* (1872) offers a collection of poems that dramatize the life of a fictional former slave, Aunt Chloe, who learns to read, becomes in involved in politics, helps build schools and churches, and works to buy a cabin for her family. Harper's novel *Iola Leroy; or, Shadows Uplifted* (1892), tells the story of an assertive young woman of mixed race who learns to stand up for her rights as an African American and as a woman. The first name of the title character was the pseudonym of the noted black journalist, antilynching advocate, and women's rights advocate Ida B. Wells-Barnett, for whom Harper was a mentor.

Active in black women's organizations, Harper was a leader of the National Woman's Christian Temperance Union from 1883 to 1890, was one of four African Americans to address the 1893 World's Congress of Representative Women at the Columbian Exposition in Chicago, and served as a founding member of the National Association of Colored Women in 1896.

Popular and critically acclaimed upon her death, on February 20, 1911, Harper received encomiums from African American activist and author W.E.B. Du Bois and from novelist and literary critic Henry James. Thereafter, however, her writing fell into neglect until a revival in the 1970s and 1980s.

Mary Ellen Snodgrass

See also: Abolitionist and Antislavery Movements; Reconstruction; Slavery and Slave Life

Sketches of Southern Life (excerpts), 1872

A collection of poems and one short story, Sketches of Southern Life *is based on Frances Ellen Watkins Harper's travels among the freed people of the South during Reconstruction. One of the preeminent works of period literature,* Sketches *evokes the central themes of Reconstruction—faith, struggle, solidarity, education, and racial uplift—from the perspective of a proud and sympathetic former slave, "Aunt Chloe." The poems presented below convey the yearning of freed blacks to elevate themselves in at least two ways, attaining literacy and worshipping in their own church.*

Learning to Read

Very soon the Yankee teachers
Came down and set up school;
But, oh! how the Rebs did hate it, –
It was agin' their rule.

Our masters always tried to hide
Book learning from our eyes;
Knowledge didn't agree with slavery –
Twould make us all too wise.

But some of us would try to steal
A little from the book,
And put the words together,
And learn by hook or crook.

I remember Uncle Caldwell,
Who took pot liquor fat
And greased the pages of his book,
And hid it in his hat.

And had his master ever seen
The leaves upon his head,
He'd have thought them greasy papers,
But nothing to be read.

And there was Mr. Turner's Ben,
    Who heard the children spell,
And picked the words right up by heart,
    And learned to read 'em well.

Well, the Northern folks kept sending
    The Yankee teachers down;
And they stood right up and helped us,
    Though Rebs did sneer and frown.

And, I longed to read my Bible,
    For precious words it said;
But when I begun to learn it,
    Folks just shook their heads,

And said there is no use trying,
    Oh! Chloe, you're too late;
But as I was rising sixty,
    I had no time to wait.

So I got a pair of glasses,
    And straight to work I went,
And never stopped till I could read
    The hymns and Testament.

Then I got a little cabin
    A place to call my own –
And I felt as independent
    As the queen upon her throne.

Church Building

Uncle Jacob often told us,
    Since freedom blessed our race
We ought all to come together
    And build a meeting place.

So we pinched, and scraped, and spared,
    A little here and there:

Though our wages was but scanty,
    The church did get a share.

And, when the house was finished,
    Uncle Jacob came to pray;
He was looking mighty feeble,
    And his head was awful gray.

But his voice rang like a trumpet;
    His eyes looked bright and young;
And it seemed a mighty power
    Was resting on his tongue.

And he gave us all his blessing –
    Twas parting words he said,
For soon we got the message
    The dear old man was dead.

But I believe he's in the kingdom,
    For when we shook his hand
He said, "Children, you must meet me
    Right in the promised land;

"For when I'm done a moiling
    And toiling here below,
Through the gate into the city
    Straightway I hope to go."

Sources: Electronic Text Center, University of Virginia (http://etext.lib.virginia.edu); Frances E. Watkins Harper, *Sketches of Southern Life* (Philadelphia: Ferguson Bros., 1891).

Harte, Bret

(1836–1902)

Journalist, author, and humorist Francis Bret Harte brought a new voice and perspective to American literature in depicting the regional color of the frontier West. His stories, poems, and articles satisfied growing popular interest in California after the Gold Rush and made him a leading force in the local-color movement in American literature.

The son of schoolteacher Henry Hart and his wife, Elizabeth Ostrander Harte, he was born on August 25, 1836, in Albany, New York, and reared in Brooklyn. The boy was fatherless from age 8 and largely unschooled, except from private reading. Before he died, his father changed the spelling of the family name from "Hart" to "Harte." Henry Harte also left his son with a love of books. Francis, or Frank, spent much of his boyhood alone, reading the Bible, Charles Dickens, and Edgar Allan Poe, among others.

In 1854, Harte set out for California, where his mother had moved and remarried. After a series of odd jobs, including teaching, mining, and guarding Wells Fargo deliveries, he got his first work in journalism on the weekly *Northern Californian* in Uniontown. In February 1860, Harte's exposé on the "indiscriminate massacre" of 100 Miyot Indians at Humboldt Bay enraged local whites, who ran him out of town.

Settling in San Francisco at age 24, Harte married Anna Griswold and began issuing a gossip column, poems, and a series of short stories for a local journal, the *Golden Era*. The first of his stories was a satire called "My Metamorphosis" (1860), about a European tourist who poses as a statue to avoid embarrassment while swimming nude. Harte's humorous works ventured into sly racial commentary in "Plain Language from Truthful James" (1860), a 60-line ballad about Ah Sin, an ostensibly naive Chinese card player who outwits two white cardsharps at euchre.

Maturation

Harte matured as a writer under the guidance of San Francisco author and intellectual Jessie Benton Frémont, the wife of military officer, explorer, and politician John C. Frémont. As a member of her abolitionist and literary salon, Harte met such leading lights as novelist Herman Melville and landscape designer Frederick Law Olmsted. Expanding his literary scope, he turned his firsthand accounts of life in the goldfields into stories featuring dialect humor, including such successes as "The Man of No Account," "M'liss," "The Work on Red Mountain," and "A Night at Wingdam." In verse, his ode "The Pony Express," published in the *Golden Era* on July 1, 1860, paid homage to "the bold Knife of the Pony Express."

Perhaps because of the demands of a wife and son, Harte picked up the pace of his writing in 1864 with the Bohemian Papers, a series covering such local topics as encroaching urbanism in "Mission Dolores" and imported coolie labor in "John Chinaman." In May 1864, he partnered with humorist Mark Twain, a reporter for the San Francisco *Morning Call* who shared Harte's disdain for European styles and topics. At age 30, Harte cofounded the *Californian,* a literary weekly that published his own reviews, topical articles, serialized novels, and a collection of Civil War verses, as well as Twain's "The Celebrated Jumping Frog of Calaveras County" (1865) and early stories and poems by Ambrose Bierce.

In 1865, Harte mourned the loss of Abraham Lincoln as an icon of the West and "the representative American." He wrote of the slain president, "His eloquence and humor partook of the local and material influences, mixed with that familiar knowledge of men and character which the easy intercourse of the pioneer had fostered." In "A Second Review of the Grand Army," published May 24, 1865, Harte composed a moving salute to the two-day parade down Pennsylvania Avenue in Lincoln's honor.

In 1867, Harte assisted Twain in refining the final manuscript of the latter's humorous travelogue *The Innocents Abroad* (1869). Twain praised his friend for quality editing and for a steady friendship that survived their fractious collaboration. In his own right, Harte parodied James Fenimore Cooper with *Muck-a-Muck* (1867) and offered a keen burlesque of Charles Dickens's *A Christmas Carol* in *The Haunted Man* (1867).

Newspaper editor, writer, and humorist Bret Harte—an early collaborator of Mark Twain—pioneered the style, subject matter, and local color of American Western writing.

Despite these successes, the era strapped Harte financially, requiring him to review plays for the *Morning Call* and to freelance Western commentary for Eastern newspapers. A satirical poem for the Springfield (Massachusetts) *Republican*, "To the Pliocene Skull" (1866), mocked the discovery in California of a reputed prehistoric fossil, the Calaveras Skull, which turned out to be a hoax. Critics charged Harte with developing a snide insider's voice for Eastern readers that condescended to the antics and pretensions of less genteel Westerners. Publication of *The Lost Galleon and Other Tales* (1867), an anthology of ballads and comic rhymes, earned Harte a comeuppance from the San Francisco *Dramatic Chronicle*, which accused him of stealing his motif, style, and tone from Robert Browning, Oliver Wendell Holmes, and John Greenleaf Whittier.

Mid-Career and Late Works

Work from Harte's mid-career far surpassed his early and late writings in quality and originality. In 1868, he began editing the *Overland Monthly,* a new literary magazine that became one of the West's prize contributions to American letters. Its pages would carry the first fiction of Jack London, the satire of Ambrose Bierce, and the egalitarian verse of Walt Whitman. The *Overland Monthly* also carried Harte's two most famous stories, "The Outcasts of Poker Flat" (1869), a sentimental tale of tolerance and forgiveness in a crumbling California town where a secret committee seeks to restore virtue and respectability by exiling "immoral" characters; and "The Luck of Roaring Camp" (1868), about the birth of a baby boy in a gold mining camp and his effect on the men who raise him. Despite the outrage of religious reviewers who considered it sacrilege, "The Luck" earned critical accolades from the Eastern literary establishment. Within the first six months of the magazine's publication, Harte's stories boosted circulation to 3,000 and extended its popularity to Nevada, Oregon, and the Atlantic seaboard. Reprints of his fiction appeared in such publications as the *Albany Evening Journal, Hartford Courant, New York Evening Post, Providence Journal,* and *Springfield Republican* and in England in *Fun* and the *Piccadilly Annual.*

To the chagrin of Anton Roman, publisher of the *Overland Monthly,* Harte insisted on truth in reporting. He refused to gloss over the San Francisco earthquake of October 21, 1868, which Roman suppressed lest the news stymie investment. While Harte's detractors considered him frivolous and aloof from the business world, he refused to retreat from presenting the real Pacific Coast experience to the outside world—as reflected in his anthology of early prose writings, *The Luck of Roaring Camp and Other Sketches* (1870).

In 1871, Harte returned East to write for the *Atlantic Monthly* in Boston, through which he befriended poets Henry Wadsworth Longfellow and James Russell Lowell. The publisher offered Harte $10,000 for 12 stories per year, the highest retainer for any American author to date. By most accounts, the quality of Harte's work went into decline. His collaboration with Twain produced a racist stage play, *Ah Sin, the Heathen Chinee* (1876), based on his earlier ballad; the play flopped. His suspense tale "At the Mission of San Carmel" (1877) recycled a biracial romance from earlier frontier writings. "The Old

Camp-Fire" (1893), a less formulaic meditation on nature, expressed Harte's regard for camaraderie among the redwoods and his dread that the telegraph and railroad endangered Western beauty.

In the final stage of his career, Harte abandoned his family, accepted consulships in Germany and Scotland, and retired to London to write for hack publishers. He died of throat cancer at Camberley, England, on May 5, 1902. A pioneer in the literature of the American West, Bret Harte is credited as one of the nation's great mythmakers, giving voice and color to nineteenth-century life in California and creating such enduring stock characters as the foul-mouthed stage driver, rough-hewn miner, noble Indian, pathetic tramp, humble Chinaman, and saloon girl with the heart of gold.

Mary Ellen Snodgrass

"The Luck of Roaring Camp," 1868

Bret Harte's short story "The Luck of Roaring Camp," published in the August 1868 issue of Overland Monthly, *of which he was also the editor, elevated the 29-year-old writer to a position of literary prominence. A parody of the welcoming of the baby Jesus by the magi and shepherds, the story is about the birth of a baby boy in a California mining settlement during the time of the Gold Rush. The boy's mother dies in childbirth, and the men of the camp decide to raise the child themselves. A sentimental tale of rough-and-tumble characters civilized by an infant child and their responsibility for him, "The Luck" is also a realistic depiction of life in a mining camp with vivid characterizations and regional color. Eight months before it was published, Harte had lost the third of his five children, a son who died unnamed a week after birth.*

There was commotion in Roaring Camp. It could not have been a fight, for in 1850 that was not novel enough to have called together the entire settlement. The ditches and claims were not only deserted, but "Tuttle's grocery" had contributed its gamblers, who, it will be remembered, calmly continued their game the day that French Pete and Kanaka Joe shot each other to death over the bar in the front room. The whole camp was collected before a rude cabin on the outer edge of the clearing. Conversation was carried on in a low tone, but the name of a woman was frequently repeated. It was a name familiar enough in the camp,—"Cherokee Sal."

Perhaps the less said of her the better. She was a coarse and, it is to be feared, a very sinful woman. But at that time she was the only woman in Roaring Camp, and was just then lying in sore extremity, when she most needed the ministration of her own sex. Dissolute, abandoned, and irreclaimable, she was yet suffering a martyrdom hard enough to bear even when veiled by sympathizing womanhood, but now terrible in her loneliness. The primal curse had come to her in that original isolation which must have made the punishment of the first transgression so dreadful. It was, perhaps, part of the expiation of her sin that, at a moment when she most lacked her sex's intuitive tenderness and care, she met only the half-contemptuous faces of her masculine associates. Yet a few of the spectators were, I think, touched by her sufferings. Sandy Tipton thought it was "rough on Sal," and, in the contemplation of her condition, for a moment rose superior to the fact that he had an ace and two bowers in his sleeve.

It will be seen also that the situation was novel. Deaths were by no means uncommon in Roaring Camp, but a birth was a new thing. People had been dismissed the camp effectively, finally, and with no possibility of return; but this was the first time that anybody had been introduced *ab initio.* Hence the excitement.

"You go in there, Stumpy," said a prominent citizen known as "Kentuck," addressing one of the loungers. "Go in there, and see what you kin do. You've had experience in them things."

Perhaps there was a fitness in the selection. Stumpy, in other climes, had been the putative head of two families; in fact, it was owing to some legal informality in these proceedings that Roaring Camp—a city of refuge—was indebted to his company. The crowd approved the choice, and Stumpy was wise enough to bow to the majority. The door closed on the extempore surgeon and midwife, and Roaring Camp sat down outside, smoked its pipe, and awaited the issue.

The assemblage numbered about a hundred men. One or two of these were actual fugitives from justice, some were criminal, and all were reckless. Physically they exhibited no indication of their past lives and character. The greatest scamp had a Raphael face, with a profusion of blonde hair; Oakhurst, a gambler, had the melancholy air and intellectual abstraction of a Hamlet; the coolest and most courageous man was scarcely over five feet in height, with a soft voice and an embarrassed, timid manner. The term "roughs" applied to them was a distinction rather than a definition. Perhaps in the minor details of fingers, toes, ears, etc., the camp may have been deficient, but these slight omissions did not detract from their aggregate force. The strongest man had but three fingers on his right hand; the best shot had but one eye.

Such was the physical aspect of the men that were dispersed around the cabin. The camp lay in a triangular valley between two hills and a river. The only outlet was a steep trail over the summit of a hill that faced the cabin, now illuminated by the rising moon. The suffering woman might have seen it from the rude bunk whereon she lay,—seen it winding like a silver thread until it was lost in the stars above.

A fire of withered pine boughs added sociability to the gathering. By degrees the natural levity of Roaring Camp returned. Bets were freely offered and taken regarding the result. Three to five that "Sal would get through with it;" even that the child would survive; side bets as to the sex and complexion of the coming stranger. In the midst of an excited discussion an exclamation came from those nearest the door, and the camp stopped to listen. Above the swaying and moaning of the pines, the swift rush of the river, and the crackling of the fire rose a sharp, querulous cry,—a cry unlike anything heard before in the camp. The pines stopped moaning, the river ceased to rush, and the fire to crackle. It seemed as if Nature had stopped to listen too.

The camp rose to its feet as one man! It was proposed to explode a barrel of gunpowder; but in consideration of the situation of the mother, better counsels prevailed, and only a few revolvers were discharged; for whether owing to the rude surgery of the camp, or some other reason, Cherokee Sal was sinking fast. Within an hour she had climbed, as it were, that rugged road that led to the stars, and so passed out of Roaring Camp, its sin and shame, forever. I do not think that the announcement disturbed them much, except in speculation as to the fate of the child. "Can he live now?" was asked of Stumpy. The answer was doubtful. The only other being of Cherokee Sal's sex and maternal condition in the settlement was an ass. There was some conjecture as to fitness, but the experiment was tried. It was less problematical than the ancient treatment of Romulus and Remus, and apparently as successful.

Above the swaying and moaning of the pines, the swift rush of the river, and the crackling of the fire rose a sharp, querulous cry.

When these details were completed, which exhausted another hour, the door was opened, and the anxious crowd of men, who had already formed themselves into a queue, entered in single file. Beside the low bunk or shelf, on which the figure of the mother was starkly outlined below the blankets, stood a pine table. On this a candle-box was placed, and within it, swathed in staring red flannel, lay the last arrival at Roaring Camp. Beside the candle-box was placed a hat. Its use was soon indicated. "Gentlemen," said Stumpy, with a singular mixture of authority and *ex officio* complacency,—"gentlemen will please pass in at the front door, round the table, and out at the back door. Them as wishes to contribute anything toward the orphan will find a hat handy." The first man entered with his hat on; he uncovered, however, as he looked about him, and so unconsciously set an example to the next. In such communities good and bad actions are catching. As the procession filed in comments were audible,—criticisms addressed perhaps rather to Stumpy in the character of showman: "Is that him?" "Mighty small specimen;" "Hasn't more'n got the color;" "Ain't bigger nor a derringer." The contributions were as characteristic: A silver tobacco box;

a doubloon; a navy revolver, silver mounted; a gold specimen; a very beautifully embroidered lady's handkerchief (from Oakhurst the gambler); a diamond breastpin; a diamond ring (suggested by the pin, with the remark from the giver that he "saw that pin and went two diamonds better"); a slung-shot; a Bible (contributor not detected); a golden spur; a silver teaspoon (the initials, I regret to say, were not the giver's); a pair of surgeon's shears; a lancet; a Bank of England note for £5; and about $200 in loose gold and silver coin. During these proceedings Stumpy maintained a silence as impassive as the dead on his left, a gravity as inscrutable as that of the newly born on his right. Only one incident occurred to break the monotony of the curious procession. As Kentuck bent over the candle-box half curiously, the child turned, and, in a spasm of pain, caught at his groping finger, and held it fast for a moment. Kentuck looked foolish and embarrassed. Something like a blush tried to assert itself in his weather-beaten cheek. "The d—d little cuss!" he said, as he extricated his finger, with perhaps more tenderness and care than he might have been deemed capable of showing. He held that finger a little apart from its fellows as he went out, and examined it curiously. The examination provoked the same original remark in regard to the child. In fact, he seemed to enjoy repeating it. "He rastled with my finger," he remarked to Tipton, holding up the member, "the d—d little cuss!"

It was four o'clock before the camp sought repose. A light burnt in the cabin where the watchers sat, for Stumpy did not go to bed that night. Nor did Kentuck. He drank quite freely, and related with great gusto his experience, invariably ending with his characteristic condemnation of the newcomer. It seemed to relieve him of any unjust implication of sentiment, and Kentuck had the weaknesses of the nobler sex. When everybody else had gone to bed, he walked down to the river and whistled reflectingly. Then he walked up the gulch past the cabin, still whistling with demonstrative unconcern. At a large redwood-tree he paused and retraced his steps, and again passed the cabin. Halfway down to the river's bank he again paused, and then returned and knocked at the door. It was opened by Stumpy. "How goes it?" said Kentuck, looking past Stumpy toward the candle-box. "All serene!" replied Stumpy. "Anything up?" "Nothing." There was a pause—an embarrassing one—Stumpy still holding the door. Then Kentuck had recourse to his finger, which he held up to Stumpy. "Rastled with it,—the d—d little cuss," he said, and retired.

The next day Cherokee Sal had such rude sepulture as Roaring Camp afforded. After her body had been committed to the hillside, there was a formal meeting of the camp to discuss what should be done with her infant. A resolution to adopt it was unanimous and enthusiastic. But an animated discussion in regard to the manner and feasibility of providing for its wants at once sprang up. It was remarkable that the argument partook of none of those fierce personalities with which discussions were usually conducted at Roaring Camp. Tipton proposed that they should send the child to Red Dog,—a distance of forty miles,—where female attention could be procured. But the unlucky suggestion met with fierce and unanimous opposition. It was evident that no plan which entailed parting from their new acquisition would for a moment be entertained. "Besides," said Tom Ryder, "them fellows at Red Dog would swap it, and ring in somebody else on us." A disbelief in the honesty of other camps prevailed at Roaring Camp, as in other places.

The introduction of a female nurse in the camp also met with objection. It was argued that no decent woman could be prevailed to accept Roaring Camp as her home, and the speaker urged that "they didn't want any more of the other kind." This unkind allusion to the defunct mother, harsh as it may seem, was the first spasm of propriety,—the first symptom of the camp's regeneration. Stumpy advanced nothing. Perhaps he felt a certain delicacy in interfering with the selection of a possible successor in office. But when questioned, he averred stoutly that he and "Jinny"—the mammal before alluded to—could manage to rear the child. There was something original, independent, and heroic about the plan that pleased the camp. Stumpy was retained. Certain articles were sent for to Sacramento. "Mind," said the treasurer, as he pressed a bag of gold-dust into the expressman's hand, "the best that can be got,—lace, you know, and filigree-work and frills,—d—n the cost!" Strange to say, the child thrived. Perhaps the invigorating climate of the mountain camp was compensation for material deficiencies. Nature took the foundling to her broader breast. In that rare atmosphere of the Sierra foothills,—that air pungent with balsamic odor, that ethereal cordial at once bracing and exhilarating,—he may have found food and nourishment, or a subtle chemistry that transmuted ass's milk to lime and phosphorus. Stumpy inclined to the belief that it was the latter and good nursing. "Me and that ass," he would say, "has been father and mother to him! Don't you," he would add, apostrophizing the helpless bundle before him, "never go back on us."

By the time he was a month old the necessity of giving him a name became apparent. He had generally been known as "The Kid," "Stumpy's Boy," "The Coyote" (an allusion to his vocal powers), and even by Kentuck's endearing diminutive of "The d—d little cuss." But these were felt to be vague and unsatisfactory, and were at last dismissed under another influence. Gamblers and adventurers are generally superstitious, and Oakhurst one day declared that the baby had brought "the luck" to Roaring Camp. It was certain that of late they had been successful. "Luck" was the name agreed upon, with the prefix of Tommy for greater convenience. No allusion was made to the mother, and the father was unknown. "It's better," said the philosophical Oakhurst, "to take a fresh deal all round. Call him Luck, and start him fair." A day was accordingly set apart for the christening. What was meant by this ceremony the reader may imagine who has already gathered some idea of the reckless irreverence of Roaring Camp. The master of ceremonies was one "Boston," a noted wag, and the occasion seemed to promise the greatest facetiousness. This ingenious satirist had spent two days in preparing a burlesque of the Church service, with pointed local allusions. The choir was properly trained, and Sandy Tipton was to stand godfather. But after the procession had marched to the grove with music and banners, and the child had been deposited before a mock altar, Stumpy stepped before the expectant crowd. "It ain't my style to spoil fun, boys," said the little man, stoutly eying the faces around him, "but it strikes me that this thing ain't exactly on the squar. It's playing it pretty low down on this yer baby to ring in fun on him that he ain't goin' to understand. And ef there's goin' to be any godfathers round, I'd like to see who's got any better rights than me." A silence followed Stumpy's speech. To the credit of all humorists be it said that the first man to acknowledge its justice was the satirist thus stopped of his fun. "But," said Stumpy, quickly following up his advantage, "we're here for a christening, and we'll have it. I proclaim you Thomas Luck, according to the laws of the United States and the State of California, so help me God." It was the first time that the name of the Deity had been otherwise uttered than profanely in the camp. The form of christening was perhaps even more ludicrous than the satirist had conceived; but strangely enough, nobody saw it and nobody laughed. "Tommy" was christened as seriously as he would have been under a Christian roof, and cried and was comforted in as orthodox fashion.

And so the work of regeneration began in Roaring Camp. Almost imperceptibly a change came over the settlement. The cabin assigned to "Tommy Luck"—or "The Luck," as he was more frequently called—first showed signs of improvement. It was kept scrupulously clean and whitewashed. Then it was boarded, clothed, and papered. The rosewood, cradle, packed eighty miles by mule, had, in Stumpy's way of putting it, "sorter killed the rest of the furniture." So the rehabilitation of the cabin became a necessity. The men who were in the habit of lounging in at Stumpy's to see "how 'The Luck' got on" seemed to appreciate the change, and in self-defense the rival establishment of "Tuttle's grocery" bestirred itself and imported a carpet and mirrors. The reflections of the latter on the appearance of Roaring Camp tended to produce stricter habits of personal cleanliness. Again Stumpy imposed a kind of quarantine upon those who aspired to the honor and privilege of holding The Luck. It was a cruel mortification to Kentuck—who, in the carelessness of a large nature and the habits of frontier life, had begun to regard all garments as a second cuticle, which, like a snake's, only sloughed off through decay—to be debarred this privilege from certain prudential reasons. Yet such was the subtle influence of innovation that he thereafter appeared regularly every afternoon in a clean shirt and face still shining from his ablutions. Nor were moral and social sanitary laws neglected. "Tommy," who was supposed to spend his whole existence in a persistent attempt to repose, must not be disturbed by noise. The shouting and yelling, which had gained the camp its infelicitous title, were not permitted within hearing distance of Stumpy's. The men conversed in whispers or smoked with Indian gravity. Profanity was tacitly given up in these sacred precincts, and throughout the camp a popular form of expletive, known as "D—n the luck!" and "Curse the luck!" was abandoned, as having a new personal bearing. Vocal music was not interdicted, being supposed to have a soothing, tranquilizing quality; and one song, sung by "Man-o'-War Jack," an English sailor from her Majesty's Australian colonies, was quite popular as a lullaby. It was a lugubrious recital of the exploits of "the Arethusa, Seventy-four," in a muffled minor, ending with a prolonged dying fall at the burden of each verse," On b-oo-o-ard of the Arethusa." It was a fine sight to see Jack holding The Luck, rocking from side to side as if with the motion of a ship, and crooning forth this naval ditty. Either through the peculiar rocking of Jack or the length of his song,—it contained ninety stanzas, and was continued with conscientious deliberation to the bitter end,—the lullaby generally had the desired effect. At such times the men would lie at full length under the trees in the soft summer twilight, smoking their pipes and drinking in the melodious utterances. An indistinct idea that this was pastoral happiness pervaded the camp. "This 'ere kind o' think," said the Cockney Simmons, meditatively reclining on his elbow, "is 'evingly." It reminded him of Greenwich.

On the long summer days The Luck was usually carried to the gulch from whence the golden store of Roaring Camp was taken. There, on a blanket spread over pine boughs, he would lie while the men were working in the ditches below. Latterly there was a rude attempt to decorate this bower with flowers and sweet-smelling shrubs, and generally some one would bring him a cluster of wild honeysuckles, azaleas, or the painted blossoms of Las Mariposas. The men had suddenly awakened to the fact that there were beauty and significance in these trifles, which they had so long trodden carelessly beneath their feet. A flake of glittering mica, a fragment of variegated quartz, a bright pebble from the bed of the creek, became beautiful to eyes thus cleared and strengthened, and were invariably put aside for The Luck. It was wonderful how many treasures the woods and hillsides yielded that "would do for Tommy." Surrounded by playthings such as never child out of fairyland had before, it is to be hoped that Tommy was content. He appeared to be serenely happy, albeit there was an infantine gravity about him, a contemplative light in his round gray eyes, that sometimes worried Stumpy. He was always tractable and quiet, and it is recorded that once, having crept beyond his "corral,"—a hedge of tessellated pine boughs, which surrounded his bed,—he dropped over the bank on his head in the soft earth, and remained with his mottled legs in the air in that position for at least five minutes with unflinching gravity. He was extricated without a murmur. I hesitate to record the many other instances of his sagacity, which rest, unfortunately, upon the statements of prejudiced friends. Some of them were not without a tinge of superstition. "I crep' up the bank just now," said Kentuck one day, in a breathless state of excitement, "and dern my skin if he wasn't a-talking to a jaybird as was a-sittin' on his lap. There they was, just as free and sociable as anything you please, a-jawin' at each other just like two cherrybums." Howbeit, whether creeping over the pine boughs or lying lazily on his back blinking at the leaves above him, to him the birds sang, the squirrels chattered, and the flowers bloomed. Nature was his nurse and playfellow. For him she would let slip between the leaves golden shafts of sunlight that fell just within his grasp; she would send wandering breezes to visit him with the balm of bay and resinous gum; to him the tall redwoods nodded familiarly and sleepily, the bumblebees buzzed, and the rooks cawed a slumberous accompaniment.

Such was the golden summer of Roaring Camp. They were "flush times," and the luck was with them. The claims had yielded enormously. The camp was jealous of its privileges and looked suspiciously on strangers. No encouragement was given to immigration, and, to make their seclusion more perfect, the land on either side of the mountain wall that surrounded the camp they duly preempted. This, and a reputation for singular proficiency with the revolver, kept the reserve of Roaring Camp inviolate. The expressman—their only connecting link with the surrounding world—sometimes told wonderful stories of the camp. He would say, "They've a street up there in 'Roaring' that would lay over any street in Red Dog. They've got vines and flowers round their houses, and they wash themselves twice a day. But they're mighty rough on strangers, and they worship an Ingin baby."

With the prosperity of the camp came a desire for further improvement. It was proposed to build a hotel in the following spring, and to invite one or two decent families to reside there for the sake of The Luck, who might perhaps profit by female companionship. The sacrifice that this concession to the sex cost these men, who were fiercely skeptical in regard to its general virtue and usefulness, can only be accounted for by their affection for Tommy. A few still held out. But the resolve could not be carried into effect for three months, and the minority meekly yielded in the hope that something might turn up to prevent it. And it did.

The winter of 1851 will long be remembered in the foothills. The snow lay deep on the Sierras, and every mountain creek became a river, and every river a lake. Each gorge and gulch was transformed into a tumultuous watercourse that descended the hillsides, tearing down giant trees and scattering its drift and debris along the plain. Red Dog had been twice under water, and Roaring Camp had been forewarned. "Water put the gold into them gulches," said Stumpy. "It's been here once and will be here again!" And that night the North Fork suddenly leaped over its banks and swept up the triangular valley of Roaring Camp.

In the confusion of rushing water, crashing trees, and crackling timber, and the darkness which seemed to flow with the water and blot out the fair valley, but little could be done to collect the scattered camp. When the morning broke, the cabin of Stumpy, nearest the river-bank, was gone. Higher up the gulch they found the body of its unlucky owner; but the pride, the hope, the joy, The Luck, of Roaring Camp had disappeared. They were returning with sad hearts when a shout from the bank recalled them.

It was a relief-boat from down the river. They had picked up, they said, a man and an infant, nearly exhausted, about two miles below. Did anybody know them, and did they belong here?

It needed but a glance to show them Kentuck lying there, cruelly crushed and bruised, but still holding The Luck of Roaring Camp in his arms. As they bent over the strangely assorted pair, they saw that the child was cold and pulseless. "He is dead," said one. Kentuck opened his eyes. "Dead?" he repeated feebly. "Yes, my man, and you are dying too." A smile lit the eyes of the expiring Kentuck. "Dying!" he repeated; "he's a-taking me with him. Tell the boys I've got The Luck with me now;" and the strong man, clinging to the frail babe as a drowning man is said to cling to a straw, drifted away into the shadowy river that flows forever to the unknown sea.

Source: Project Gutenberg (www.gutenberg.org); Bret Harte, *The Luck of Roaring Camp and Other Tales* (Boston: Houghton Mifflin, 1902).

Howe, Julia Ward

(1819–1910)

A prominent New England abolitionist, social reformer, and poet, Julia Ward Howe is best known for her lyrics to the "Battle Hymn of the Republic," which inspired Union forces during the Civil War and remains a popular patriotic song to the present day.

A native of New York City, she was born on May 27, 1819, to Samuel Ward, a successful Wall Street banker, and Julia Rush Cutler, a published poet. Reared by governesses after the death of her mother in 1824, she spent her childhood studying Greek and Romance languages with tutors and attended a private school on Fifth Avenue. Reading in the home library, she taught herself math and science—which were excluded from the curriculum of female students—and immersed herself in philosophy, the classics, and contemporary European literature. Thoughtful, independent-minded, and aspiring to the life of a writer, she abandoned her father's puritanical Calvinism for Unitarianism, began writing verse, and submitted original criticism to the *Literary and Theological Review* and the *New York Review.*

In early 1843, she met and married physician and reformer Samuel Gridley Howe, who was 18 years her senior. She called him "Chev" for his honorary title of chevalier in the Greek Revolution during the 1820s. The couple lived in Boston, where Samuel Howe had founded the New England Asylum for the Blind (later the Perkins School for the Blind), the first institution of its kind in America. The couple would have six children together, from 1844 to 1858.

In 1851, Samuel also helped found the *Daily Commonwealth,* a leading abolitionist journal, which he edited for the next two years with Julia's assistance. In the meantime, unknown to her husband, she was composing personal spiritual verse that appeared in her first published collection, *Passion-Flowers,* in December 1853. Reflecting her desire for a career outside the home, which her husband flatly opposed, one poem in the collection, "The Heart's Astronomy," acknowledged her ambivalence toward motherhood and her yearning for intellectual liberation.

In 1856, her five-act play *Leonora, or the World's Own* pondered questions of gender identity and self-assertion on the stage in New York and Boston. The Howes' marriage remained stormy, as Julia struggled for the independence, respect, and understanding that conventional morality denied to most women in nineteenth-century America.

Exceedingly well-read and fluent in seven languages, Howe developed friendships with many of Boston's intellectual elite, including fellow Unitarians and abolitionists William Ellery Channing, Thomas Wentworth Higginson, and Theodore Parker. In 1860, with the conflict over slavery pushing the nation to the brink of war, she became a particular admirer of radical abolitionist William Lloyd Garrison and an active participant in the Underground Railroad.

On November 18, 1861, with the war under way, Julia and Samuel Howe visited Washington, D.C., to review Union troops and to meet President Abraham Lincoln at the White House. Inspired by the visit—and encouraged by traveling companion and abolitionist James Freeman Clarke to write a soldiers' song to the tune of "John Brown's Body"—she penned the lyrics to "Battle Hymn of the Republic" early the next morning at the Willard Hotel. The lines, she later recalled, "began to twine themselves in my mind." In the predawn light, she sprang out of bed and "scrawled the verses almost without looking at the paper."

Published in the February 1862 issue of *The Atlantic Monthly,* Howe's lyrics looked to God for victory rather than to weapons, military strategy, or combat heroics. "Battle Hymn of the Republic" quickly became one of the most popular songs of the Union cause among soldiers and civilians alike. At a critical moment in the war for the North, Union prisoners in Richmond, Virginia, sang the anthem to celebrate the victory at Gettysburg on July 3, 1863. Later in the year, Howe returned to Washington to visit the wounded and to rally the Army of the Potomac. Admirers thrust copies of the anthem at her for autographs.

After the war, Howe continued her efforts on behalf of social reform, specifically the causes of women's rights and pacifism. In 1868, she joined the Reverend Olympia Brown and Lucy Stone in founding the New England Woman Suffrage Association, the nation's first suffrage organization. Months later, however, a schism with Susan B. Anthony and Elizabeth Cady Stanton allied Howe with the more moderate wing of the movement. In 1869, with Stone, the Reverend Henry Ward

Beecher, Antoinette Brown Blackwell, and Henry Brown Blackwell, Howe cofounded the American Woman Suffrage Association (AWSA), which supported enfranchisement for women at the state level and promoted passage of the Fifteenth Amendment to grant the vote to black males. (Anthony and Stanton founded the rival National Woman Suffrage Association, which favored federal enfranchisement and opposed the Fifteenth Amendment because it did not include women.) From 1872 to 1879, Howe assisted Stone and Henry Brown Blackwell in editing *Woman's Journal,* an influential women's rights weekly.

Upon her husband's death in 1876, Howe wrote in her diary, "Start my new life today." In the decades that followed, she traveled the world to promote women's rights, peace, prison reform, and education while continuing to write, study, and help lead such organizations as the Association of American Women, New England Women's Club, and AWSA. She published a total of four books of poetry during her lifetime, as well as travel sketches and a biography of Transcendentalist editor and intellectual Margaret Fuller.

At Howe's death, from pneumonia on October 17, 1910, at age 91, more than 4,000 mourners gathered at her memorial service in Boston. In 1908, she had become the first woman elected to the American Academy of Arts and Letters.

Mary Ellen Snodgrass

See also: Abolitionist and Antislavery Movements

"Battle Hymn of the Republic," 1862

Poet Julia Ward Howe was inspired to write the lyrics to the "Battle Hymn of the Republic," a popular Union anthem during the Civil War, by a visit to a military camp near Washington, D.C., in November 1861. She later remembered that the lines came to her almost intact as she awoke the next morning. The original five stanzas appeared on the front page of The Atlantic Monthly *in February 1862; the chorus and sixth verse were added later. The hymn is sung to the tune of "John Brown's Body."*

Mine eyes have seen the glory of the coming of the Lord
He is trampling out the vintage where the grapes of wrath are stored;
He hath loosed the fateful lightning of His terrible swift sword:
His truth is marching on.

Glory, glory, hallelujah!
Glory, glory, hallelujah!
Glory, glory, hallelujah!
His truth is marching on.

I have seen Him in the watch-fires of a hundred circling camps,
They have builded Him an altar in the evening dews and damps;
I can read His righteous sentence by the dim and flaring lamps:
His day is marching on.

Glory, glory, hallelujah!
Glory, glory, hallelujah!
Glory, glory, hallelujah!
His day is marching on.

I have read a fiery gospel writ in burnished rows of steel:
"As ye deal with my contemners, so with you my grace shall deal;
Let the Hero, born of woman, crush the serpent with his heel,
Since God is marching on."

Glory, glory, hallelujah!
Glory, glory, hallelujah!
Glory, glory, hallelujah!
Since God is marching on.

He has sounded forth the trumpet that shall never call retreat;
He is sifting out the hearts of men before His judgment-seat:
Oh, be swift, my soul, to answer Him! be jubilant, my feet!
Our God is marching on.

Glory, glory, hallelujah!
Glory, glory, hallelujah!
Glory, glory, hallelujah!
Our God is marching on.

In the beauty of the lilies Christ was born across the sea,
With a glory in his bosom that transfigures you and me:
As he died to make men holy, let us die to make men free,
While God is marching on.

Glory, glory, hallelujah!
Glory, glory, hallelujah!
Glory, glory, hallelujah!
While God is marching on.

He is coming like the glory of the morning on the wave,
He is Wisdom to the mighty, He is Succour to the brave,
So the world shall be His footstool, and the soul of Time His slave,
Our God is marching on.

Glory, glory, hallelujah!
Glory, glory, hallelujah!
Glory, glory, hallelujah!
Our God is marching on.

Jacobs, Harriet

(1813–1897)

Providing a firsthand female perspective on human bondage, activist and teacher Harriet Ann Jacobs escaped sexual enslavement and published a memoir of a mother's life on the run. Her 1861 autobiography, *Incidents in the Life of a Slave Girl,* published under the pen name Linda Brent, eventually became the most widely read slave narrative by a female author.

The mulatto granddaughter of a white planter, she was born on February 11, 1813, in Edenton, North Carolina. Harriet and her younger brother John were the slaves of their mother's owner, tavern keeper John Horniblow and his wife, Margaret, who taught her reading, spelling, and needlework. After the death of her mother, Delilah Horniblow, in 1819, Harriet worked from age 6 into her preteens as a house servant to the family. Upon Margaret's death in 1825, she bequeathed Harriet to her 3-year-old niece, Mary Matilda Norcom. The girl's father, Edenton physician James Norcom, became Harriet's effective master. Harriet soon recognized him as a sexual predator.

At age 15, Harriet succeeded in evading Norcom's advances, but he refused to let her wed a freedman carpenter. Desperate to escape her master and despised by Norcom's jealous wife, Harriet took refuge in a secret affair with a white attorney and North Carolina legislator named Samuel Tredwell Sawyer. She bore two children from that relationship, Joseph S. Jacobs in 1829 and Louisa Matilda Jacobs in 1833. According to her later account, Norcom threatened to ship the children away if she continued to refuse his advances. Reaching her breaking point, Harriet devised a plan. By running away, she reasoned, she could induce Norcom to sell the children to their father and thereby save them from the life of plantation slaves. With the help of an Underground Railroad transporter, Jacobs fled the Norcom plantation in June 1835.

After taking refuge in a nearby swamp, she hid herself in an attic crawl space at her grandmother's house in Edenton. Remaining in that "little dismal hole" for the next seven years, she read the Bible, sewed, and kept an eye on her children. Sawyer, who had purchased the children according to her wishes, was elected to the U.S. House of Representatives in 1837 and moved to Washington, D.C. Although he did not free Joseph or Louisa at the time, he later made arrangements for them to move north. Neither of them knew of their mother's whereabouts, or even if she was still alive.

Jacobs finally left North Carolina in 1842, escaping by steamer to New Haven, Connecticut, and then by train to Boston. At age 31, she reunited with her children and secured a place for the three of them to live together in Boston, where she worked as a nursemaid for the family of poet and editor Nathaniel Parker Willis. Aware that Norcom had made several attempts to track her down, however, Jacobs was forced to stay on the move. In 1849, she relocated to Rochester, New York, where she made friends with libertarian William Cooper Nell and Quaker antislavery agents Amy Kirby Post and Isaac Post. Living with Amy's parents for a year, Jacobs had her children educated in local schools.

After passage of the Fugitive Slave Law of 1850, Quaker abolitionists Cornelia Grinnell Willis and Nathaniel Willis paid $300 to free Jacobs from Norcom's persecution. Publisher Lydia Maria Child, editor of the *National Anti-Slavery Standard,* and Amy Post assisted Jacobs with her autobiography, which she began writing in 1853. Jacobs excerpted some of the episodes in Horace Greeley's *New York Tribune,* but the scenes of sexual stalking offended public taste and publication ceased. A Boston publisher issued the memoir in book form in 1861, followed by a British edition titled *The Deeper Wrong; Or, Incidents in the Life of a Slave Girl.* Long mistaken for a novel by a white author, Jacobs's memoir was obscured by the advent of war and remained largely unread for more than a century.

During the Civil War, Jacobs served as a nurse and teacher to black soldiers and refugees and as a placement worker for orphans in Alexandria, Virginia, and Savannah, Georgia. After operating a boardinghouse near the Harvard University campus in the 1870s, Jacobs retired to her daughter Louisa's home in Washington, D.C., where she died on March 7, 1897. Based on research in the 1970s and 1980s, literary historian Jean Fagan Yellin uncovered the real identity of Linda Brent's pseudonymous memoir and confirmed the veracity of the account. *Incidents in the Life of a Slave Girl* earned the acclaim of modern critics and historians as one of the great slave narratives, providing unique insights into the fear and degradation faced by the female slave population.

Mary Ellen Snodgrass

See also: Abolitionist and Antislavery Movements; Slavery and Slave Life

◇◇

Chapter 18, "Months of Peril," *Incidents in the Life of a Slave Girl,* 1861

◇◇

Though it remained obscure and largely unread for more than a century after initial publication, Harriet Jacobs's Incidents in the Life of a Slave Girl *became a classic of the slave narrative and the most widely read work of its kind by a woman. Aside from the sexual harassment and abuse she faced as a young adult, Jacobs's narrative is extraordinary for its account of her seven years in hiding, the fear and anxiety that dogged her even after escape to the North, and the joyous reunification with her children. For all the dark experiences it describes,* Incidents in the Life *is a story of personal fortitude and triumph. Jacobs published her account under the pseudonym Linda Brent and changed the names of the other characters. In Chapter 18, she has fled the plantation, her slave master (Dr. Flint) has offered a $300 reward for her capture, and the search for her continues. From her initial hiding place, Linda moves to a thicket in the swamp and finally to the attic of her grandmother's house. Benny and Ellen are her son Joseph and daughter Louisa, and William is her brother John.*

> The search for me was kept up with more perseverence than I had anticipated. I began to think that escape was impossible. I was in great anxiety lest I should implicate the friend who harbored me. I knew the consequences would be frightful; and much as I dreaded being caught, even that seemed better than

causing an innocent person to suffer for kindness to me. A week had passed in terrible suspense, when my pursuers came into such close vicinity that I concluded they had tracked me to my hiding-place. I flew out of the house, and concealed myself in a thicket of bushes. There I remained in an agony of fear for two hours. Suddenly, a reptile of some kind seized my leg. In my fright, I struck a blow which loosened its hold, but I could not tell whether I had killed it; it was so dark, I could not see what it was; I only knew it was something cold and slimy. The pain I felt soon indicated that the bite was poisonous. I was compelled to leave my place of concealment, and I groped my way back into the house. The pain had become intense, and my friend was startled by my look of anguish. I asked her to prepare a poultice of warm ashes and vinegar, and I applied it to my leg, which was already much swollen. The application gave me some relief, but the swelling did not abate. The dread of being disabled was greater than the physical pain I endured. My friend asked an old woman, who doctored among the slaves, what was good for the bite of a snake or a lizard. She told her to steep a dozen coppers in vinegar, over night, and apply the cankered vinegar to the inflamed part.

I had succeeded in cautiously conveying some messages to my relatives. They were harshly threatened, and despairing of my having a chance to escape, they advised me to return to my master, ask his forgiveness, and let him make an example of me. But such counsel had no influence with me. When I started upon this hazardous undertaking, I had resolved that, come what would, there should be no turning back. "Give me liberty, or give me death," was my motto. When my friend contrived to make known to my relatives the painful situation I had been in for twenty-four hours, they said no more about my going back to my master. Something must be done, and that speedily; but where to return for help, they knew not. God in his mercy raised up "a friend in need."

Among the ladies who were acquainted with my grandmother, was one who had known her from childhood, and always been very friendly to her. She had also known my mother and her children, and felt interested for them. At this crisis of affairs she called to see my grandmother, as she not unfrequently did. She observed the sad and troubled expression of her face, and asked if she knew where Linda was, and whether she was safe. My grandmother shook her head, without answering. "Come, Aunt Martha," said the kind lady, "tell me all about it. Perhaps I can do something to help you." The husband of this lady held many slaves, and bought and sold slaves. She also held a number in her own name; but she treated them kindly, and would never allow any of them to be sold. She was unlike the majority of slaveholders' wives. My grandmother looked earnestly at her. Something in the expression of her face said "Trust me!" and she did trust her. She listened attentively to the details of my story, and sat thinking for a while. At last she said, "Aunt Martha, I pity you both. If you think there is any chance of Linda's getting to the Free States, I will conceal her for a time. But first you must solemnly promise that my name shall never be mentioned. If such a thing should become known, it would ruin me and my family. No one in my house must know of it, except the cook. She is so faithful that I would trust my own life with her; and I know she likes Linda. It is a great risk; but I trust no harm will come of it. Get word to Linda to be ready as soon as it is dark, before the patrols are out. I will send the housemaids on errands, and Betty shall go to meet Linda." The place where we were to meet was designated and agreed upon. My grandmother was unable to thank the lady for this noble deed; overcome by her emotions, she sank on her knees and sobbed like a child.

I received a message to leave my friend's house at such an hour, and go to a certain place where a friend would be waiting for me. As a matter of prudence no names were mentioned. I had no means of conjecturing who I was to meet, or where I was going. I did not like to move thus blindfolded, but I had no choice. It would not do for me to remain where I was. I disguised myself, summoned up courage to meet the worst, and went to the appointed place. My friend Betty was there; she was the last person I expected to see. We hurried along in silence. The pain in my leg was so intense that it seemed as if I should drop but fear gave me strength. We reached the house and entered unobserved. Her first words were: "Honey, now you is safe. Dem devils ain't coming to search *dis* house. When I get you into missis' safe place, I will bring some nice hot supper. I specs you need it after all dis skeering." Betty's vocation led her to think eating the most important thing in life. She did not realize that my heart was too full for me to care much about supper.

The mistress came to meet us, and led me up stairs to a small room over her own sleeping apartment. "You will be safe here, Linda," said she; "I keep this room to store away things that are out of use. The girls are not accustomed to be sent to it, and they will not suspect any thing unless they hear some noise. I always keep it locked, and Betty shall take care of the key. But you must be very careful, for my sake as well as your own; and you must never tell my secret; for it would ruin me and my family. I will keep the girls busy in the morning, that Betty may have a chance to bring your breakfast; but it will not do for her to come to you again till night. I will come to see you sometimes. Keep up your courage. I hope this state of things will not last long." Betty came with the "nice hot supper," and the mistress hastened down stairs to keep things straight till she returned. How my heart overflowed with gratitude! Words choked in my throat; but I could have kissed the feet of my benefactress. For that deed of Christian womanhood, may God forever bless her!

I went to sleep that night with the feeling that I was for the present the most fortunate slave in town. Morning came and filled my little cell with light. I thanked the heavenly Father for this safe retreat. Opposite my window was a pile of feather beds. On the top of these I could lie perfectly concealed, and command a view of the street through which Dr. Flint passed to his office. Anxious as I was, I felt a gleam of satisfaction when I saw him. Thus far I had outwitted him, and I triumphed over it. Who can blame slaves for being cunning? They are constantly compelled to resort to it. It is the only weapon of the weak and oppressed against the strength of their tyrants.

I was daily hoping to hear that my master had sold my children; for I knew who was on the watch to buy them. But Dr. Flint cared even more for revenge than he did for money. My brother William and the good aunt who had served in his family twenty years, and my little Benny, and Ellen, who was a little over two years old, were thrust into jail, as a means of compelling my relatives to give some information about me. He swore my grandmother should never see one of them again till I was brought back. They kept these facts from me for several days. When I heard that my little ones were in a loathsome jail, my first impulse was to go to them. I was encountering dangers for the sake of freeing them, and must I be the cause of their death? The thought was agonizing. My benefactress tried to soothe me by telling me that my aunt would take good care of the children while they remained in jail. But it added to my pain to think that the good old aunt, who had always been so kind to her sister's orphan children, should be shut up in prison for no other crime than loving them. I suppose my friends feared a reckless movement on my part, knowing, as they did, that my life was bound up in my children. I received a note from my brother William. It was scarcely legible, and ran thus: "Wherever you are, dear sister, I beg of you not to come here. We are all much better off than you are. If you come, you will ruin us all. They would force you to tell where you had been, or they would kill you. Take the advice of your friends; if not for the sake of me and your children, at least for the sake of those you would ruin."

Who can blame slaves for being cunning? It is the only weapon of the weak and oppressed against the strength of their tyrants.

Poor William! He also must suffer for being my brother. I took his advice and kept quiet. My aunt was taken out of jail at the end of a month, because Mrs. Flint could not spare her any longer. She was tired of being her own housekeeper. It was quite too fatiguing to order her dinner and eat it too. My children remained in jail, where brother William did all he could for their comfort. Betty went to see them sometimes, and brought me tidings. She was not permitted to enter the jail; but William would hold them up to the grated window while she chatted with them.

When she repeated their prattle, and told me how they wanted to see their ma, my tears would flow. Old Betty would exclaim, "Lors, chile! what's you crying 'bout? Dem young uns vil kill you dead. Don't be so chick'n hearted! If you does, you vil nebber git thro' dis world."

Good old soul! She had gone through the world childless. She had never had little ones to clasp their arms round her neck; she had never seen their soft eyes looking into hers; no sweet little voices had called her mother; she had never pressed her own infants to her heart, with the feeling that even in fetters there was something to live for. How could she realize my feelings? Betty's husband loved children dearly, and wondered why God had denied them to him. He expressed great sorrow when he came to Betty with the tidings that Ellen had been taken out of jail and carried to Dr. Flint's. She had the measles a short time before they carried her to jail, and the disease had left her eyes affected. The doctor had taken her home to attend to them. My children had always been afraid of the doctor and his wife. They had never been inside of their house. Poor little Ellen cried all day to be carried back to prison. The instincts of childhood are true. She knew she was loved in the jail. Her screams and sobs annoyed Mrs. Flint. Before night she called one of the slaves, and said, "Here, Bill, carry this brat back to the jail. I can't stand her noise. If she would be quiet I should like to keep the little minx. She would make a handy waiting-maid for my daughter by and by. But if she staid here, with her white face, I suppose I should either kill her or spoil her. I hope the doctor will sell them as far as wind and water can carry them. As for their mother, her ladyship will find out yet what she gets by running away. She hasn't so much feeling for her children as a cow has for its calf. If she had, she would have come back long ago, to get them out of jail, and save all this expense and trouble. The good-for-nothing hussy! When she is caught, she shall stay in jail, in irons, for one six months, and then be sold to a sugar plantation. I shall see her broke in yet. What do you stand there for, Bill? Why don't you go off with the brat? Mind, now, that you don't let any of the niggers speak to her in the street!"

When these remarks were reported to me, I smiled at Mrs. Flint's saying that she should either kill my child or spoil her. I thought to myself there was very little danger of the latter. I have always considered it as one of God's special providences that Ellen screamed till she was carried back to jail.

That same night Dr. Flint was called to a patient, and did not return till near morning. Passing my grandmother's, he saw a light in the house, and thought to himself, "Perhaps this has something to do with Linda." He knocked, and the door was opened. "What calls you up so early?" said he. "I saw your light, and I thought I would just stop and tell you that I have found out where Linda is. I know where to put my hands on her, and I shall have her before twelve o'clock." When he had turned away, my grandmother and my uncle looked anxiously at each other. They did not know whether or not it was merely one of the doctor's tricks to frighten them. In their uncertainty, they thought it was best to have a message conveyed to my friend Betty. Unwilling to alarm her mistress, Betty resolved to dispose of me herself. She came to me, and told me to rise and dress quickly. We hurried down stairs, and across the yard, into the kitchen. She locked the door, and lifted up a plank in the floor. A buffalo skin and a bit of carpet were spread for me to lie on, and a quilt thrown over me. "Stay dar," said she, "till I sees if dey know 'bout you. Dey say dey vil put thar hans on you afore twelve o'clock. If dey *did* know whar you are, dey won't know *now.* Dey'll be disapinted dis time. Dat's all I got to say. If dey comes rummagin 'mong *my* tings, de'll get one bressed sarssin from dis 'ere nigger." In my shallow bed I had but just room enough to bring my hands to my face to keep the dust out of my eyes; for Betty walked over me twenty times in an hour, passing from the dresser to the fireplace. When she was alone, I could hear her pronouncing anathemas over Dr. Flint and all his tribe, every now and then saying, with a chuckling laugh, "Dis nigger's too cute for 'em dis time." When the housemaids were about, she had sly ways of drawing them out, that I might hear what they would say. She would repeat stories she had heard about my being in this, or that, or the other place. To which they would answer, that I was not fool enough to be staying round there; that I was in Philadelphia or New York before this time. When all were abed and asleep, Betty raised the plank, and said, "Come out, chile; come out. Dey don't know nottin 'bout you. Twas only white folks' lies, to skeer de niggers."

Some days after this adventure I had a much worse fright. As I sat very still in my retreat above stairs, cheerful visions floated through my mind. I thought Dr. Flint would soon get discouraged, and would be willing to sell my children, when he lost all hopes of making them the means of my discovery. I knew who was ready to buy them. Suddenly I heard a voice that chilled my blood. The sound was too familiar to me, it had been too dreadful, for me not to recognize at once my old master. He was in the house, and I at once concluded he had come to seize me. I looked round in terror. There was no way of escape. The voice receded. I supposed the constable was with him, and they were searching the house. In my alarm I did not forget the trouble I was bringing on my generous benefactress. It seemed as if I were born to bring sorrow on all who befriended me, and that was the bitterest drop in the bitter cup of my life. After a while I heard approaching footsteps; the key was turned in my door. I braced myself against the wall to keep from falling. I ventured to look up, and there stood my kind benefactress alone. I was too much overcome to speak, and sunk down upon the floor.

"I thought you would hear your master's voice," she said; "and knowing you would be terrified, I came to tell you there is nothing to fear. You may even indulge in a laugh at the old gentleman's expense. He is so sure you are in New York, that he came to borrow five hundred dollars to go in pursuit of you. My sister had some money to loan on interest. He has obtained it, and proposes to start for New York to-night. So, for the present, you see you are safe. The doctor will merely lighten his pocket hunting after the bird he has left behind."

Source: Linda Brent, *Incidents in the Life of a Slave Girl* (Boston, 1861).

Lincoln, Abraham

(1809–1865)

The accomplishments that have made Abraham Lincoln a venerated figure in national lore are familiar to most Americans: As the sixteenth president of the United States from March 1861 to his assassination in April 1865, he balanced the plight of slaves against the danger of a sundered Union by ending human bondage while winning the Civil War. In the aftermath of his martyrdom, a popular memorial print titled *Apotheosis of Lincoln* depicted the slain president rising to heaven, where he is welcomed with open arms by George Washington. The United States at the time was a predominantly Christian nation, and it was easy for most Americans to associate the two men in biblical terms. Allegorically, Washington was God the Creator—the man who had fashioned the new nation out of darkness; Lincoln was Jesus the Savior—the man who had redeemed the nation from its sins.

In their state of shock and sadness, Americans in 1865 might be forgiven for elevating this man of humble origins and consummate humility to immortal status. To this day, however, Americans link Lincoln and Washington in the national mythology. At least in Lincoln's case, the many reasons for this no doubt include the *words* he wrote and spoke. Regarded as the most gifted writer among all U.S. presidents, he has been referred to as "the Mark Twain of American politics." As a prose stylist, he stands alongside such contemporary giants as Emerson, Melville, and Thoreau. But beyond the writings of even these literary lions, Lincoln's words had a direct and profound influence on the affairs of state, the lives of millions of Americans, and the course of history. From his famous "House Divided" speech and debates with Senator Stephen Douglas in 1858 to his Cooper Union speech on slavery in February 1860, his inaugural addresses of 1861 and 1865, and the immortal Gettysburg Address in November 1863, Lincoln's words transformed public life in America—permanently.

"For Lincoln," wrote historian and journalist Fred Kaplan in his book *Lincoln: The Biography of a Writer* (2008), "words mattered immensely. His increasing skill in their use during his lifetime, and his high valuation of their power, mark him as the one president who was both a national leader and a genius with language at a time when its power and integrity mattered more than it does today. His was a personality and a career forged in the crucible of language."

Youth

"It is great folly to attempt to make anything out of me or my early life," Lincoln would write as a presidential candidate. "It can all be condensed into a single sentence; and that sentence you will find in Gray's *Elegy:* 'The short and simple annals of the poor.' "

The son of farmer Thomas Lincoln and Nancy Hanks Lincoln—both illiterates—he was born on February 12, 1809, in Hardin County, Kentucky. The Lincolns belonged to a Baptist congregation that had separated from another church because of its opposition to slavery. When Lincoln was 2 years old, his father moved the family 10 miles north to a farm on Knob Creek; Lincoln would speak fondly of that place for the rest of his life. When he was 7, Lincoln's father moved the family to southern Indiana in search of more fertile farmland and, according to the future president, free soil.

Following the death of their mother in 1818 and their father's remarriage in 1819, Abraham, his brother Thomas, and their older sister Sarah grew up primarily under the care of a beloved stepmother, Sarah Bush Lincoln. Young Abraham worked for his father but detested farm labor, a fact that contributed to their strained relationship. Despite receiving scarcely a year of formal schooling, Lincoln was much more interested in books. While living in Indiana, he occasionally hired himself out as a laborer; at 19, he was hired to ride a flatboat of goods down the Mississippi River to New Orleans. By this time, Lincoln had grown into a strong, tall, lanky youth. In an age when the average American man stood 5 feet, 6 inches tall, Lincoln towered above his peers at 6 feet, 4 inches.

Early Career

In 1830, Thomas Lincoln moved the family again, this time to the banks of the Sangamon River near present-day Decatur, Illinois. Abraham, then 21, went along and stayed with the family until making a second flatboat trip to New Orleans. It was during this trip that he witnessed firsthand the dehumanizing effects of slavery. In 1831, he struck out on his own and moved to the village of New Salem, Illinois, where he found work as a store clerk.

Lincoln enlisted in a local militia during the Black Hawk War of 1832, but his company did not see any action and Lincoln returned to New Salem by June of that year. After running unsuccessfully for the Illinois General Assembly in the fall, he worked in town as a shopkeeper, surveyor, and postmaster. Running again for a seat in the legislature in 1834, he won election as a Whig. While serving in the Assembly for four terms (1834–1841), he also began studying law on his own. After gaining admission to the Illinois bar in March 1837, he left New Salem and moved to Springfield to begin his legal career.

Once established in Springfield, Lincoln entered into law practice with John T. Stuart, who had encouraged him to take up the law. Stuart was also a cousin of Mary Ann Todd, a Kentuckian whom Lincoln met in December 1839 while she was living with a sister in Springfield. Despite a sometimes rocky relationship, including a broken engagement, the couple was married on November 4, 1842. They would have four sons, of whom the eldest, Robert Todd Lincoln, was the only one to survive to adulthood. In the meantime, with law partner William H. Herndon, Lincoln built a successful practice in Springfield, solidified connections in the Whig Party, and, at Herndon's urging, became an increasingly staunch opponent of slavery.

With the party process at the time calling for rotating offices among loyal Whigs, it was Lincoln's turn to run for the U.S. House of Representatives in 1846. He won the election easily in a heavily Whig district and spent a single, mostly unhappy, term in Congress. Following the party leadership, he opposed the Mexican-American War (1846–1848), accusing the James K. Polk administration and the Democratic Party of fabricating the conflict in order to acquire more territory for the expansion of slavery. Despite the unpopularity of his war views among Illinois Democrats, Congressman Lincoln voted for the Wilmot Proviso, which would have prohibited slavery in any territory acquired from Mexico. Compounding his disappointment in Washington was Mary's distaste for the city and her early return to Illinois with the children. Having pledged to serve only one term, Lincoln returned to Springfield when his term expired in 1849. There, for the next five years, he rode the trails of the Eighth Circuit, making a respectable living at the law.

Emergence as a National Figure

Inevitably, perhaps, it was the issue of slavery that brought Lincoln back into public life. Specifically, it was passage of the proslavery Kansas-Nebraska Act in May 1854. Effectively repealing the Missouri Compromise of 1820, the legislation called for "popular sovereignty" on the issue of slavery in the two Western territories, meaning that residents would have the opportunity to vote on whether to allow slavery in their territories. Aside from breaching the Missouri Compromise, argued Lincoln and others, granting popular sovereignty in Kansas and Nebraska opened other Western territories to the possibility of slavery.

Stirred to action, Lincoln declared his opposition to slavery in a speech in October 1854 and ran for a U.S. Senate seat in 1855, unsuccessfully. The following year, he joined the new Republican Party and finished second in balloting for the vice-presidential nomination. Despite these setbacks, Lincoln was beginning to gain recognition as a compelling voice against the spread of slavery. Capitalizing on his growing reputation in Illinois, he decided to make another run for the U.S. Senate in 1858, this time against incumbent Stephen A. Douglas, the chief architect of the Kansas-Nebraska Act and champion of popular sovereignty. This time, Lincoln won the Republican nomination, which he accepted with his famous House Divided speech at the state capitol on June 16, 1858. "A house divided against itself cannot stand," he declared. "I believe this government cannot endure permanently half slave and half free. . . . It will become all one thing, or all the other."

In a series of seven debates across Illinois, Lincoln railed against Douglas's views on popular sovereignty and the expansion of slavery. The consensus at the time held that Lincoln had gotten the best of Douglas in the debates, but voters that fall gave a majority of seats in the legislature to the Democratic Party. Because U.S. senators were chosen by the state legislature, Douglas was returned to office. On the strength of Lincoln's strong showing, however, his reputation in Illinois and across the country continued to grow. He began to be mentioned as a possible Republican presidential candidate in 1860.

Run for the White House

The turning point in Lincoln's quest for the presidency was another speech, at Cooper Union in New York City on February 27, 1860. Taking a staunch antislavery position on moral grounds, he told the crowd: "Let us have faith that might makes right, and in that faith let us, to the end, dare to do our duty as we understand it." The New York press covered the speech extensively and reprinted it in several newspapers. Lincoln, already popular in Illinois and the West, now made a strong impression on the Eastern Republican establishment.

That May, as the party held its national convention in Chicago, Lincoln remained in Springfield, awaiting the outcome of nomination balloting. Foremost among his rivals were Senator William H. Seward of New York, generally regarded as the frontrunner, and Salmon P. Chase, a former governor of Ohio. With many members of the party concerned that both Seward and Chase were too radical in their opposition to slavery and risked losing the Western states, the mainstream turned to Lincoln as a compromise candidate. He won the nomination on the third ballot, with Hannibal Hamlin of Maine selected as his running mate. The party platform at the convention called for restrictions on the expansion of slavery, implementation of a protective tariff, passage of a homestead bill, and construction of a transcontinental railroad—all unpopular in South.

Lincoln ran against three opponents in the November election: his old nemesis Douglas, Vice President John C. Breckinridge, and former senator John Bell of Tennessee. Douglas and Breckinridge represented separated factions within the divided Democratic Party, while Bell ran as a third-party candidate on the Constitutional Union ticket. The campaign revolved around the expansion of slavery. While Southerners feared that Lincoln was a "Black Republican" who would abolish slavery immediately upon taking office, the Illinoisan reasserted his years-long position: he opposed the spread of slavery to new territories but let it stand where already in place.

The power of words helped make Abraham Lincoln a leader for the ages. His Gettysburg Address and Second Inaugural Address are inscribed in the Lincoln Memorial.

With the Democratic vote split between Douglas and Breckinridge, Lincoln won the presidency handily on November 6, 1860. His 1.85 million popular votes represented just under 40 percent of all ballots cast. His margin of victory was even stronger in the Electoral College, where he captured 180 of 303 votes. Ominously, however, not a single electoral vote came from the South; indeed, in most Southern states, he did not even appear on the ballot.

Lincoln's election set the nation firmly on the course of civil war. On December 20, just 10 weeks before his inauguration, South Carolina became the first state to secede from the Union. Six more followed before his swearing in on March 4, 1861.

Presidency

Lincoln's presidency forever changed the course of American history. By the time of his assassination at the hands of Southern partisan John Wilkes Booth on April 14, 1865, more than 600,000 Americans had died in the Civil War, slavery had been abolished, homesteaders and railroad builders were developing millions of acres of frontier land, and the American presidency was more powerful than ever before. As commander in chief, Lincoln urged his generals to fight, replaced them when they delayed, and took an active part in making military strategy. As a politician, he expanded the powers of the presidency and marshaled the talents of his cabinet to preserve the Union and advance his legislative agenda in Congress. As a statesman and moral force, he succeeded in the paramount objective of freeing the slaves without leaving the nation permanently divided.

Achieving that dual objective required both the strength and tenacity of waging war for four years and the wisdom and timing to choose the right moment for claiming the high moral ground. On September 22, 1862, five days after Union forces fended off a Confederate invasion of Maryland in the Battle of Antietam, Lincoln issued the Emancipation Proclamation. To take effect on January 1, 1863, the presidential order proclaimed that all slaves in Confederate territory would be free forever. In reality, because most Southern states were still in rebellion and because the order did not apply to border states fighting for the Union, the Proclamation actually freed few men and women in bondage. While it also sanctioned the use of black recruits in the Union army, its greatest import lay in the implicit declaration, to both sides and the rest of the world, that the eradication of slavery was no less a goal of the war federal war effort than was reunification of the republic. As throughout Lincoln's life in politics, the words alone had a profound transformational effect. They were a source of inspiration for the Union cause and African Americans on both sides of the Mason-Dixon Line; a justification for the heavy war casualties being suffered; an effective warning to European powers that had considered fighting on the side of the Confederacy; and the beginning of the end of the Southern plantation system.

Upon Lincoln's death on April 15, 1865, Secretary of War Edwin M. Stanton famously remarked, "Now he belongs to the ages." More human than godlike, Lincoln is still revered as the savior of the Union and, in the view of many historians, America's greatest president. His efforts to ensure that government "of the people, by the people, and for the people shall not perish from the earth"—underscored by his rise from humble roots—makes certain that his place in American memory will be, as Stanton predicted, secure for the ages.

Jeff Hacker and Benjamin T. Arrington

See also: Gettysburg Address; Whitman, Walt

Second Inaugural Address, 1865

By Abraham Lincoln's second inauguration as president on March 4, 1865, the Civil War was drawing to a close and his dual mission of preserving the Union and ending slavery was nearing attainment. In his inaugural address, however, Lincoln struck a chord of reconciliation rather than triumph, setting the tone for a lenient, pragmatic, even compassionate approach to Reconstruction. Six weeks later, Lincoln lay dead. Today, visitors to the Lincoln Memorial in Washington, D.C., can find the words of his Second Inaugural Address inscribed on the interior of the north wall.

Fellow Countrymen:

At this second appearing to take the oath of the presidential office there is less occasion for an extended address than there was at the first. Then a statement, somewhat in detail, of a course to be pursued seemed fitting and proper. Now, at the expiration of four years, during which public declarations have been constantly called forth on every point and phase of the great contest which still absorbs the attention and engrosses the energies of the nation, little that is new could be presented. The progress of our arms, upon which all else chiefly depends, is as well known to the public as to myself, and it is, I trust, reasonably satisfactory and encouraging to all. With high hope for the future, no prediction in regard to it is ventured.

On the occasion corresponding to this four years ago all thoughts were anxiously directed to an impending civil war. All dreaded it; all sought to avert it. While the inaugural address was being delivered from this place, devoted altogether to saving the Union without war, insurgent agents were in the city seeking to destroy it without war—seeking to dissolve the Union and divide effects by negotiation. Both parties deprecated war, but one of them would make war rather than let the nation survive, and the other would accept war rather than let it perish, and the war came.

One-eighth of the whole population were colored slaves, not distributed generally over the Union, but localized in the southern part of it. These slaves constituted a peculiar and powerful interest. All knew that this interest was somehow the cause of war. To strengthen, perpetuate, and extend this interest was the object for which the insurgents would rend the Union even by war, while the Government claimed no right to do more than to restrict the territorial enlargement of it. Neither party expected for the war the magnitude or the duration which it has already attained.

Neither anticipated that the cause of the conflict might cease with or even before the conflict itself should cease. Each looked for an easier triumph, and a result less fundamental and astounding. Both read the same Bible and pray to the same God, and each invokes His aid against the other. It may seem strange that any men should dare to ask a just God's assistance in wringing their bread from the sweat of other men's faces, but let us judge not, that we be not judged. The prayers of both could not be answered. That of neither has been answered fully. The Almighty has His own purposes. "Woe unto the world because of offenses; for it must needs be that offenses come, but woe to that man by whom the offense cometh." If we shall suppose that American slavery is one of those offenses which, in the providence of God, must needs come, but which, having continued through His appointed time, He now wills to remove, and that He gives to both North and South this terrible war as the woe due to those by whom the offense came, shall we discern therein any departure from those divine attributes which the believers in a living God always ascribe to Him? Fondly do we hope, fervently do we pray, that this mighty scourge of war may speedily pass away. Yet, if God wills that it continue until all the wealth piled by the bondsman's two hundred and fifty years of unrequited toil shall be sunk, and until every drop of blood drawn with the lash shall be paid by another drawn with the sword, as was said three thousand years ago, so still it must be said "the judgments of the Lord are true and righteous altogether."

With malice toward none, with charity for all, with firmness in the right as God gives us to see the right, let us strive on to finish the work we are in, to bind up the nation's wounds, to care for him who shall have borne the battle and for his widow and his orphan, to do all which may achieve and cherish a just and lasting peace among ourselves and with all nations.

Source: Abraham Lincoln Papers at the Library of Congress, Manuscript Division.

Muir, John

(1838–1914)

Scottish-born naturalist, conservationist, and author John Muir devoted his life to exploring, observing, and protecting the great wilderness areas of the United States. His crusading efforts and extensive writings—books, essays, and letters—exposed millions of Americans to the majestic beauty of the nation's natural environment and the importance of preserving it. The founder of the Sierra Club, one of the preeminent conservation organizations in the United States, and instrumental in the creation of the nation's first federally designated park areas, he has been called the father of both the conservation movement and the National Park System.

Muir was born on April 21, 1838, in Dunbar, Scotland, to Ann Gilrye and Daniel Muir, a staunch Calvinist who insisted that his children memorize Bible passages. At age 11, Muir emigrated with his family to a homestead at Portage, Wisconsin, where they adopted a simple, antimaterialist lifestyle. Self-taught by readings in the works of explorers Alexander von Humboldt and Mungo Park, Muir became an avid naturalist, imbued with intellectual curiosity and independent thought. He also developed a skill at whittling wood, exhibiting clocks, locks, pendulums, thermometers, and barometers at the 1860 Wisconsin State Fair.

After two years studying botany and geology at the University of Wisconsin at Madison, Muir taught school briefly in nearby McKeebey. In 1863, he abandoned the goal of studying medicine and avoided participation in the Civil War by taking the first of a lifelong series of walking tours, exploring Illinois and Iowa. To avoid the military draft, he fled to Meaford, Canada, on Lake Huron, where a fire destroyed his field journals. Returning to the United States in 1866, he found work as an efficiency consultant at a wagon-wheel factory in Indianapolis, Indiana, but his future as a mechanical engineer was cut short by a machine accident in which he nearly lost sight in one eye. He resolved to follow his dream of natural exploration.

In September 1867, armed with a volume of Robert Burns's verse, Muir embarked on a life of wandering America's wildernesses. He began with a 1,000-mile hike to survey the length of the Mississippi River and to view the Cumberland range in Tennessee, the Hiwassee River in the Carolinas, and the Chattahoochee Forest of northern Georgia. His postwar musings on Union general William Tecumseh Sherman's devastation of the South drew parallels between the human suffering and the plight of old trees, "those aged, half-consumed, and fallen parents who bear in sad measure the ineffaceable marks of the farthest-reaching and most infernal of all civilized calamities." Muir's pilgrimage eventually took him to Fernandina, Florida, and the swamps of Cedar Key, where he spent two months recuperating from the effects of malaria and typhoid fever. His observations on the journey were later published as *A Thousand Mile Walk to the Gulf* (1916).

Venturing up the Pacific Coast in 1868, Muir reached San Francisco in March and soon set out for the Sierra Nevada of eastern California, his home for the next six years. Trekking more than 200 miles from San Francisco, he arrived at the Yosemite Valley in July 1869 and was awestruck by the setting. He likened its serenity and majesty to that of a natural temple, which became a central metaphor of his later memoir, *My First Summer in the Sierra* (1911). Muir settled in the valley to herd sheep in Tuolumne Meadows, operate a ferry, and study the ecosystems of Cathedral Peak, Mount Dana, and Mono Lake. As an employee of artist James Mason Hutchings, he lived in a cabin on Yosemite Falls Trail along Yosemite Creek, where he operated a water-powered sawmill, guided hikers, and entertained outsiders with his storytelling.

Muir began his career in nature writing in September 1871 with an article on glaciers for the *New York Tribune*. He followed with 12 books and some 300 articles for *The Atlantic Monthly, Harper's, The Century Magazine, Overland Monthly,* the *San Francisco Evening Bulletin, Scribner's Monthly,* and *World's Work,* including an eyewitness account of the Lone Pine earthquake on March 26, 1872. Between hikes to Mount Whitney, Mount Shasta, and Kings River Canyon, he received visitors who shared his enthusiasm for the environment and corresponded with botanist Asa Gray. On his own schedule,

Muir took extended expeditions across the Sierras, making detailed notes and sketches of plant life and geology.

Influenced by the essays of Ralph Waldo Emerson, Henry David Thoreau, and Charles Darwin, Muir celebrated a philosophy of nature that viewed humankind in perspective among buffalo wallows, verdant forests, bee pastures, granite slides, and sea squalls. He especially admired California's Digger Indians for living in close harmony with nature.

For nearly a decade after returning to society in 1878, Muir cultivated a large orchard with his wife, horticulturist Louisa Strentzel Muir, in Martinez, California. Thereafter, the livelihood from their fruit trees enabled him to devote his energies entirely to conservation and writing. Combined with the efforts of journalist Robert Underwood Johnson, two of Muir's articles on the beauty of the natural landscape and the importance of protecting wilderness areas led to passage of a bill in 1890 that established the Yosemite and Sequoia national parks, albeit still controlled by the State of California.

Two years later, again at Johnson's urging, Muir and a group of other California conservationists founded the San Francisco–based Sierra Club, dedicated to protecting the Sierra Nevada and other wilderness areas. The founders elected Muir as president, a position he held until his death. In 1897, when commercial interests threatened to dismantle the forest reserves established earlier, Muir wrote a series of magazine articles that swayed public opinion toward a national preservation policy. He also played a critical role in meeting the Sierra Club's goal of transferring control of Yosemite from state to federal authority, which Muir facilitated by escorting President Theodore Roosevelt for a visit in 1903; the transfer was completed in 1906.

In his last major battle, however, Muir failed in his efforts to stop Gifford Pinchot, the head of the U.S. Forest Service, from implementing a controversial "resource management" plan that entailed the flooding of California's Hetch Hetchy Valley, which Muir deemed sacred, and the construction of a dam. In retaliation, the Sierra Club pushed for creation of the National Park Service to wrest responsibility for the parks from the Forest Service. That came to pass in 1916, though Muir did not live to see it. He had died from pneumonia on December 24, 1914.

Mary Ellen Snodgrass

"The Yosemite," Diary Entry, 1869

John Muir's My First Summer in the Sierra, *published in 1911, was based on original diary entries from his trek in California's Sierra Nevada mountain range in 1869. A 31-year-old Scottish immigrant at the time, Muir was so enthralled by the natural beauty he encountered that he devoted his life to the conservation and preservation of the American wilderness. His diary entry for July 15, 1869—"a most memorable day of days"—recounts his first visit to the Yosemite Valley.*

July 15. —Followed the Mono Trail up the eastern rim of the basin nearly to its summit, then turned off southward to a small shallow valley that extends to the edge of the Yosemite, which we reached about noon, and encamped. After luncheon I made haste to high ground, and from the top of the ridge on the west side of Indian Cañon gained the noblest view of the summit peaks I have ever yet enjoyed. Nearly all the upper basin of the Merced was displayed, with its sublime domes and cañons, dark upsweeping forests, and glorious array of white peaks deep in the sky, every feature glowing, radiating beauty that pours into our flesh and bones like heat rays from fire. Sunshine over all; no breath of wind to stir the brooding calm. Never before had I seen so glorious a landscape, so boundless an affluence of sublime mountain beauty. The most extravagant description I might give of this view to any one who has not seen similar landscapes with his own eyes would not so much as hint its grandeur and the spiritual glow that covered it. I shouted and gesticulated in a wild burst of ecstasy, much to the astonishment of St. Bernard Carlo, who came running up to me, manifesting in his intelligent eyes a puzzled concern that was very ludicrous, which had the effect of bringing me to my senses. A brown bear, too, it would seem, had been a spectator of the show I had made of myself, for I had gone but a few yards when I started one from a thicket of brush. He evidently considered me dangerous, for he ran away very fast, tumbling over the tops of the tangled manzanita bushes in his haste. Carlo drew back, with his ears depressed as if afraid, and kept looking me in the face, as if expecting me to pursue and shoot, for he had seen many a bear battle in his day.

Following the ridge which made a gradual descent to the south, I came at length to the brow of that massive cliff that stands between Indian Cañon and Yosemite Falls, and here the far-famed valley came suddenly into view throughout almost its whole extent. The noble walls—sculptured into endless variety of domes and gables, spires and battlements and plain mural precipices—all a-tremble with the thunder tones of the falling water. The level bottom seemed to be dressed like a garden, —sunny meadows here and there, and groves of pine and oak; the river of Mercy sweeping in majesty through the midst of them and flashing back the sunbeams. The great Tissiack, or Half-Dome, rising at the upper end of the valley to a height of nearly a mile, is nobly proportioned and life-like, the most impressive of all the rocks, holding the eye in devout admiration, calling it back again and again from falls or meadows, or even the mountains beyond, —marvelous cliffs, marvelous in sheer dizzy depth and sculpture, types of endurance. Thousands of years have they stood in the sky exposed to rain, snow, frost, earthquake and avalanche, yet they still wear the bloom of youth.

The most extravagant description I might give of this view … would not so much as hint its grandeur and the spiritual glow that covered it.

I rambled along the valley rim to the westward; most of it is rounded off on the very brink, so that it is not easy to find places where one may look clear down the face of the wall to the bottom. When such places were found, and I had cautiously set my feet and drawn my body erect, I could not help fearing a little that the rock might split off and let me down, and what a down—more than three thousand feet. Still my limbs did not tremble, nor did I feel the least uncertainty as to the reliance to be placed on them. My only fear was that a flake of the granite, which in some places showed joints more or less open and running parallel with the face of the cliff, might give way. After withdrawing from such places, excited with the view I had got, I would say to myself, "Now don't go out on the verge again." But in the face of Yosemite scenery cautious remonstrance is vain; under its spell one's body seems to go where it likes with a will over which we seem to have scarce any control.

After a mile or so of this memorable cliff work I approached Yosemite Creek, admiring its easy, graceful, confident gestures as it comes bravely forward in its narrow channel, singing the last of its mountain songs on its way to its fate—a few rods more over the shining granite, then down half a mile in snowy foam to another world, to be lost in the Merced, where climate, vegetation, inhabitants, all are different. Emerging from its last gorge, it glides in wide lace-like rapids down a smooth incline into a pool where it seems to rest and compose its gray, agitated waters before taking the grand plunge, then slowly slipping over the lip of the pool basin, it descends another glossy slope with rapidly accelerated speed to the brink of the tremendous cliff, and with sublime, fateful confidence springs out free in the air.

I took off my shoes and stockings and worked my way cautiously down alongside the rushing flood, keeping my feet and hands pressed firmly on the polished rock. The booming, roaring water, rushing past close to my head, was very exciting. I had expected that the sloping apron would terminate with the perpendicular wall of the valley, and that from the foot of it, where it is less steeply inclined, I should be able to lean far enough out to see the forms and behavior of the fall all the way down to the bottom. But I found that there was yet another small brow over which I could not see, and which appeared to be too steep for mortal feet. Scanning it keenly, I discovered a narrow shelf about three inches wide on the very brink, just wide enough for a rest for one's heels. But there seemed to be no way of reaching it over so steep a brow. At length, after careful scrutiny of the surface, I found an irregular edge of a flake of the rock some distance back from the margin of the torrent. If I was to get down to the brink at all that rough edge, which might offer slight finger holds, was the only way. But the slope beside it looked dangerously smooth and steep, and the swift roaring flood beneath, overhead, and beside me was very nerve-trying. I therefore concluded not to venture farther, but did nevertheless. Tufts of artemisia were growing in clefts of the rock near by, and I filled my mouth with the bitter leaves, hoping they might help to prevent giddiness. Then, with a caution not known in ordinary circumstances, I crept down safely to the little ledge, got my heels well planted on it, then shuffled in a horizontal direction twenty or thirty feet until close to the outplunging current, which, by the time it had descended thus far, was already white. Here I obtained a perfectly free view down into the heart of the snowy, chanting throng of comet-like streamers, into which the body of the fall soon separates.

While perched on that narrow niche I was not distinctly conscious of danger. The tremendous grandeur of the fall in form and sound and motion, acting at close range, smothered the sense of fear, and in such places one's body takes keen care for safety on its own account. How long I remained down there, or how I returned, I can hardly tell. Anyhow I had a glorious time, and got back to camp about dark, enjoying triumphant exhilaration soon followed by dull weariness. Hereafter I'll try to keep from such extravagant, nerve-straining places. Yet such a day is well worth venturing for. My first view of the High Sierra, first view looking down into Yosemite, the death song of Yosemite Creek, and its flight over the vast cliff, each one of these is of itself enough for a great life-long landscape fortune—a most memorable day of days—enjoyment enough to kill if that were possible.

Source: John Muir, *My First Summer in the Sierra* (Boston: Houghton Mifflin, 1911).

Reconstruction

The term "Reconstruction" in American history refers both to the political process by which the former Confederate states were readmitted into the Union after the Civil War and to the 12-year period during which the reintegration took place—from the end of the war in April 1865 to the early days of the Rutherford B. Hayes administration in 1877. One of the defining elements of this turbulent era was the absorption of millions of former slaves into Southern society and the establishment of their rights as free men and women of the United States. The status and rights of former slaves were established by the Thirteenth, Fourteenth, and Fifteenth amendments to the U.S. Constitution, referred to collectively as the Reconstruction Amendments (ratified 1865–1870). Given the calamity of the war and the sweeping transformations it engendered, the period of Reconstruction can be understood as a true rebirth of the nation. As a political process, however, Reconstruction is regarded by many historians as a grand failure.

Notable literary works of and about Reconstruction focus primarily on the experiences of former slaves in adjusting to their freedom and in reconciling their identities as freed men and women with their established ways of life, means of subsistence, and cultural traditions. Prominent in this regard are such firsthand accounts as Frances Ellen Watkins Harper's *Sketches of Southern Life* (1872), a collection of poems and one short story based on her travels among the freed people of the South, and Elizabeth Keckley's *Behind the Scenes, or, Thirty Years a Slave and Four Years in the White House* (1868), the autobiography of a woman who rose from slavery in St. Louis to become the dressmaker and personal confidante of first lady Mary Todd Lincoln. Other authors who produced important works during this period, if markedly different in theme and setting, include Louisa May Alcott, Bret Harte, John Muir, and Mark Twain.

Wartime Initiatives

Political and social reconstruction efforts began as early as August 1861 with the signing of the Confiscation Act, which granted the federal government authority to confiscate land or property, including slaves, being used to promote Confederate independence. In the later stages of the war, as Union forces conquered new Confederate territory, Northern missionaries traveled south to establish schools and churches for former slaves.

During the period 1863–1865, the formal terms of reunification became a subject of intense debate between President Abraham Lincoln and Northern politicians. With his so-called Ten-Percent Plan in December 1863, Lincoln proposed a general amnesty for Southern whites who accepted the abolition of slavery and swore fealty to the Union; state governments would be restored after 10 percent of the prewar population within each state agreed to conditions. Radical Republicans, led by Senator Benjamin Wade of Ohio and Representative Henry Winter Davis of Maryland, called for stricter terms, such as the exclusion of all former Confederates from state and federal government after the war. By early 1864, Arkansas, Louisiana, and Tennessee had accepted the Ten-Percent Plan, but Radical Republicans refused the president's strategy and ousted Southern electees from the House of Representatives.

On July 2, 1864, both houses of Congress passed a more radical Reconstruction plan, the Wade-Davis bill, which required a majority of 1860 voters to swear loyalty to the Union as a condition of state readmission; in addition, state constitutions would have to be redrafted to end slavery and to strip Confederate political and military leaders of voting privileges. Lincoln rejected the punitive tone and substance of the bill with a pocket veto.

On March 3, 1865, a month before the end of the war, Congress established the federal Bureau of Refugees, Freedmen, and Abandoned Lands to ease the transition from bondage to citizenship for 4 million blacks and to assist in the reunion of slave families. Under the purview of the War Department, the bureau's staff of 900 agents offered immediate food and shelter, medical treatment, literacy training, and job counseling to former slaves. The Freedmen's Bureau Act also empowered officers to appropriate Confederate estates in Arkansas, Georgia, Louisiana, South Carolina, and Tennessee for use by 30,000 black farm villagers.

During Reconstruction, the Freedmen's Bureau spent $5 million in federal funds to open schools for former slaves. Formal education had been forbidden to them.

Policies and Responses

President Andrew Johnson, who acceded to the White House on April 15, 1865, following the assassination of Lincoln, was a Democrat, a staunch unionist, and a Southerner (from Tennessee), but he took only a slightly harder line toward Reconstruction than his predecessor. According to Johnson's plan, only the richest slaveholders would be barred from running for office. Above all, he hoped for a speedy process of reunification.

In December 1865, Radical Republicans controlling Congress, led by Senator Charles Sumner of Massachusetts and Representative Thaddeus Stevens of Pennsylvania, formally rejected President Johnson's lenient plan of reconciliation because of the refusal of Southern states to ratify the Thirteenth Amendment or to honor the voting rights of black males.

In April 1866, congressional passage of the Civil Rights Act over President Johnson's veto guaranteed federal protection of black citizenship rights and hearkened the beginning of Radical Reconstruction. In July, ratification of the Fourteenth Amendment trumped the right of states to deprive blacks of citizenship via "Black Codes" or other racial discrimination at the polls. A violent outbreak in New Orleans that August, which resulted in the stabbing, shooting, or beating of hundreds of blacks, gave the lie to President Johnson's belief that the nation had achieved postwar reconciliation.

Republicans seized well over two-thirds of congressional seats in the midterm elections of 1866 and promptly proposed a more rigorous Reconstruction program, which placed 15,000 federal troops across the South and suppressed the authority of recalcitrant states. The adamancy of the former rebel states resulted in the passage of four Reconstruction Acts in 1867–1868, which put Southern state governments under the control of the U.S. military. The former Confederacy (excluding Tennessee) was divided into five military districts, each under the command of a Union general. In addition, the former Confederate states were required to draft a new constitution, ratify the Fourteenth Amendment, and grant voting rights to black men.

Meanwhile, African Americans were seizing the new opportunities brought on by Reconstruction. They formed religious denominations in which they held leadership positions and worked with Northern missionaries to help former slaves, young and old, live autonomous lives. Many freedmen remained in the South and worked as independent wage laborers to secure their financial futures. Others took advantage of the Homestead Act of 1866, which made it possible to move west and claim land. Ex-slaves also began to stake a claim in elective politics, as federal troops stationed in the South made it possible for them to exercise the franchise, and as they began running for local, state, and national office, often successfully. From 1870 to 1876, according to historian Eric Foner, a total of 633 African Americans served as state legislators, 15 as U.S. congressmen, and two as U.S. senators (Hiram Rhodes Revels and Blanche Kelso Bruce, both of Mississippi).

Further altering Southern politics was the arrival of Northerners called carpetbaggers, who gained leverage in Republican Reconstruction politics with the backing of black voters and won election to state office in large numbers. While the aim of many was personal financial gain, the carpetbaggers exerted direct influence on the course of Reconstruction by shaping the new constitutions of several former Confederate states.

Federal authority and the intrusion of Yankees aroused deep hostility among white Southerners, exceeded only by the anger and resistance they felt over the loss of their slave property, the defeat of their values and way of life, and the granting of citizenship and voting rights to blacks. By the early 1870s, whites in many parts of the former Confederacy were in virtual rebellion against the outside authorities and the changes they had imposed. Secret societies such as the Ku Klux Klan terrorized blacks, and any whites perceived as supporting them, with increasing frequency throughout the South. The rising tide of atrocities finally led to passage of the Ku Klux Klan Act of 1871, signed into law by President Ulysses S. Grant, which made such offenses a federal crime and authorized the president to suspend habeas corpus in affected areas and send in federal troops.

Because of the requirements for readmission imposed by Congress on individual states, Reconstruction did not end all at once across the South. Of the 11 former Confederate states placed under military rule, eight had been readmitted to congressional representation and had reestablished Democratic control of state government by early 1876. The remaining three—Florida, Louisiana, and South Carolina—were not restored to the Union until the Compromise of 1877, which broke a three-month deadlock between Democrat Samuel J. Tilden and Republican Rutherford B. Hayes in the presidential election of November 1876. The last federal occupation forces were demobilized from the South in March 1877.

Assessment and Legacy

By most historians' accounts, Reconstruction was a tumultuous political process that failed in some of its basic goals. Aside from exploitation by carpetbaggers, violence on the part of white supremacists, and other immediate consequences, racial and sectional divisions were set for the next century and longer, blacks remained second-class citizens, and areas of the South fell into enduring poverty.

Nevertheless, the 12 years following Appomattox did bring the "new birth of freedom" anticipated by Abraham Lincoln in his Gettysburg Address, restoring the United States as a unified sovereign nation in which the abomination of slavery was eradicated and

African Americans were accorded full citizenship. With the issue of national indivisibility finally settled, many statesmen now looked to spread American economic and political influence across the globe. After the purchase of Alaska in 1867 and the unification of North and South 10 years later, government and business leaders began looking across the Pacific Ocean in search of new domains. Reconstructed, the nation embarked on a voyage to imperial greatness in the decades that followed.

Troy Kickler and Mary Ellen Snodgrass

See also: Grant, Ulysses S.; Harper, Frances Ellen Watkins; Lincoln, Abraham

Slavery and Slave Life

With African American slaves making up a significant and highly visible share of the nation's workforce, the life and culture of the slave population were defining elements of American society throughout the early republic and antebellum periods. Aside from casting the United States into moral and political turmoil that culminated in civil war, the presence of African slaves shaped the national character and regional cultures in profound and enduring ways. For slaves themselves, the quality and contours of daily life were determined by such personal factors as age, gender, and background and by the location and conditions of enslavement. As conditions varied from region to region, decade to decade, and owner to owner, the life and culture of the slave population were just as diverse. No experience of slavery could refute James Madison's characterization of the institution as America's "original sin."

Expansion, Growth, and Institutional Change

With most of the Northern states abolishing slavery gradually or completely by the first decade of the nineteenth century, the "peculiar institution" became a virtual Southern state monopoly. But the matter was far from settled. Ongoing territorial acquisition and Western settlement perpetuated the sectional dispute and triggered rounds of political deal-making. The Missouri Compromise of 1820 restricted the expansion of slavery to the Louisiana Purchase territory south of Missouri. Under the Compromise of 1850, the fate of slavery in territories entering the Union would be determined by popular sovereignty. Thus, by 1860, slavery expanded beyond the Mississippi River as far west as Texas. Territorial expansion helped fuel the growth of the U.S. slave population even after Congress banned the transatlantic slave trade, as of January 1, 1808. The total jumped from 1.1 million in 1810, to 2.5 million in 1840, to nearly 4 million in 1860.

In the South, Eli Whitney's patent of the cotton gin in 1793 had launched an economic and social revolution. By mechanically removing the sticky green seeds nestled inside cotton bolls, Whitney's device made the cultivation of short-staple cotton far less expensive and far more profitable. At the same time, mechanized textile production in the early Industrial Revolution accelerated international demand for the fiber. As a result, farmers poured into the fertile alluvial land of the Mississippi River Delta and the region known as the Black Belt—from southeastern North Carolina across much of the Lower South—to grow cotton. Harvesting the crops remained highly labor intensive, however, which increased the demand for slaves far above the number needed to support tobacco, indigo, and rice farming in colonial times.

Slave owners in Upper South states, such as Maryland and Virginia, had long complained about the cost of maintaining a slave population whose growth had outpaced the labor needs for the region's tobacco, wheat, and hemp crops. Because American-born black slaves who spoke English and understood regional farming practices commanded much higher prices than newly arrived Africans, masters in the Upper South began selling their surplus slaves to meet demand in the Lower South. Historians estimate that nearly 1 million slaves from the Upper South were forced to migrate south or west as part of the interstate slave trade, or with a master who chased the cotton dream. As a result, the share of slaves living in the Upper South declined from about 75 percent of the national total in 1790 to 39 percent in 1860. By contrast, the Lower South saw its share of the enslaved population rise from just under 20 percent to just over 60 percent during the same period. In the process, thousands of African American families were torn apart.

The domestic slave trade effectively provided masters who desired greater income with an incentive to sell their slaves, while giving owners who struggled with debt, declining fortunes, or troublesome slaves a convenient solution. The domestic slave trade also influenced the shape of African American families throughout the South. In some instances, masters encouraged their slaves to have children—which then could be sold—and offered rewards such as reduced workloads for mothers who bore numerous babies. In rarer instances, masters forced couples into sexual union in an effort to produce children with marketable physical characteristics. Far more common were planters who restricted slave marriages to persons they owned so as to retain the property rights to any children.

While the breakup of families had always been a feature of slave life, the cotton boom made the problem worse. With slaveholders starting new plantations farther west and south, many slaves not only were separated from their families but also removed from their communities. Compounding the dislocation was the fact that profit-seeking planters drove their slaves especially hard to carve out fields and raise crops on the frontier. Thus, the words "I'll sell you down the river" or "I'll put you in my pocket" sent chills down the spine of any slave.

Field Hands

Although the cotton boom in the Lower South transformed slavery in a number of ways, it did not change the fundamental activity of slave life—work. During the antebellum era, 90 percent of the U.S. slave population lived in rural areas, and a vast majority performed agricultural labor. Half of the slaves in rural areas lived and worked on plantations with 20 or more slaves; the other half labored on smaller yeoman-owned farms. As of 1860, more than 70 percent of all slaveholders in America owned fewer than 10 slaves. Thus, while large-scale plantation agriculture became a commonplace depiction in modern popular culture, it was the real experience of only about half the slave population and only a handful of slave owners. Large plantations, it was true, were far more prevalent in the Lower South than in the Upper South.

Slaves everywhere lived by the agricultural calendar and the rising and setting of the sun, working from "can see to can't." Field hands generally planted food and cash crops in the spring, weeded or thinned plants in the summer, harvested cash and food crops in the fall, and handled the maintenance needs of the farm or plantation in the winter. Short-staple cotton was the most common cash crop, as well as tobacco, wheat, and hemp in the Upper South and rice and sugarcane in the Lower South. Corn was the most widely grown food crop.

Most slaves entered fieldwork at the age of 12 and continued until they no longer could perform the work. Once they became unable

Slaves everywhere lived by the agricultural calendar and the rising and setting of the sun, working from "can see to can't."

to do fieldwork, older slaves were utilized in some other capacity, such as tending animals, caring for children, or performing domestic service. Men and women experienced relative gender equality in the fields, expected to labor side by side and to maintain an equivalent pace. Plowing usually was reserved for men, but physically capable women could be put to the plow as well.

Whether working in gangs or individual tasks, field hands spent days picking cotton in 90-degree heat, stooping from plant to plant; plucking worms from tobacco plants by hand; wading through dank-smelling, mosquito-infested water to tend delicate rice plants; or gathering and cutting sugarcane to feed the mills that operated around the clock at harvest time. When slowed by exhaustion, illness, pregnancy, or resentment, field slaves felt the sting of a whip at the hands of masters working beside them in the field or, in bigger operations, white overseers.

Domestic and Skilled Slaves

Domestic and skilled slaves tended to work on large plantations or were among the 10 percent of slaves living in an urban environment. Only the wealthiest slave owners could afford to house, feed, and clothe labor dedicated to the comfort of the household and its guests. In New York and other Northern cities after the American Revolution, the wealthy elite viewed a retinue of household slaves as a sign of prestige.

Urban and rural domestic servants filled a variety of roles, serving as cooks, maids, doormen, coachmen, gardeners, seamstresses, and nannies. They often lived in the "big house" and, as the most public face of slavery, usually were better clothed and fed than field hands. Living in close proximity to their owners, domestic servants were more assimilated into white culture than field hands, had higher rates of literacy, and formed closer personal ties with their masters. Indeed, a disproportionate number of domestic slaves were of mixed racial ancestry and, at times, were quite evidently members of the master's own family.

While domestic slaves enjoyed material benefits superior to those of field hands, they were on call 24 hours a day. Close contact with their masters meant that they could just as easily incur an owner's wrath for a mistake as they could receive praise for faithful service. Like Harriet Jacobs of Edenton, North Carolina, female slaves working in the household faced additional burdens, as some adult and adolescent males seized on their proximity to rape them or coerce them into sexual relations. In short, serving in the big house could be a position of privilege, familiarity, and less physically demanding work for some. For others, it was an environment devoid of privacy, filled with tension, and marked by violence.

Skilled slaves and artisans made up a highly specialized class of slaves whose talents made plantations more self-sufficient or allowed their owners to earn money year-round outside agriculture. Except for women who performed such domestic tasks as cooking, sewing, spinning and weaving, and basketry, skilled slaves and artisans were almost exclusively male. Valued trades included masonry, carpentry, blacksmithing, coopering, and caulking; millers, joiners, wheelwrights, and ironworkers also were prized. Skilled slaves helped build many fine Southern homes, including the White House in Washington, D.C., and produced noteworthy decorative features, such as the renowned iron gates and balconies of Charleston and New Orleans.

Hiring out slaves became a lucrative source of income for some masters, particularly in or near urban areas. By 1860 in Richmond, Virginia, for example, tobacco-processing facilities and other factories rented hundreds of slaves on a full-time or seasonal basis, reflecting the adaptability and flexibility of slavery as a labor system. Hired-out slaves could perform virtually any form of labor needed by U.S. employers. In some cases, slave labor was so cost competitive that white tradesmen sought to bar slaves from competing with them for work.

Because many of these trades required special skill and a high degree of precision, more than a few slave artisans were either taught to read and write or became literate through exposure to diagrams, business ledgers, orders, and other written documents. Most masters controlled how much their skilled slaves worked and earned, but some of the latter, such as Frederick Douglass, were allowed to hire out their own time and keep their earnings beyond a certain amount. In some cases, skilled slaves even earned enough money to purchase their freedom.

Improving Conditions

All in all, material conditions improved discernibly for American slaves from the late eighteenth to mid-nineteenth century. By this time, relationships between most masters and slaves had been shaped by at least one or two generations of American-born ancestors. Familiarity or kinship helped minimize owner indifference toward slaves and frame the ethic of planter paternalism. According to this view, slavery was a God-ordained institution in which faithful service to the owner would be rewarded with benevolent guidance and material sufficiency. Paternalism, in theory, required masters to know their bondsmen and to supervise all aspects of slave life to ensure that physical and spiritual needs were met from cradle to grave. The desire to portray themselves as benevolent gave rise to plantation rituals in which owners personally doled out food and clothing, conducted wedding services, and presented Christmas gifts to their slaves.

Further contributing to the well-being of slaves—and serving the ideal of paternalism—was the closing of the transatlantic slave trade in 1808, which made the abuse of bondsmen a risk to the owner's investment. With the curtailment of importation, slave prices rose steadily in the decades that followed, making it more costly and difficult to replace injured or overworked laborers. Moreover, by the 1830s, as the organized abolitionist movement began publicizing the most heinous aspects of slavery, slaveholders came to understand that the failure to police their own affairs provided abolitionists with further ammunition.

As a result of these factors, as well as the increased productivity and economic prosperity of the South, slave conditions by 1860 were markedly improved since the colonial era. That said, violence, abuse, and degradation still ran rampant in a system that granted owners virtually unchecked power over the lives of human chattel. The few state laws passed to protect slaves in any way were rarely enforced, with bondsmen afraid to report violations and slaveholders or overseers loath to report other whites lest their own affairs be subjected to scrutiny.

Housing, Food, and Clothing

In slave housing, the greatest improvement was the abandonment of colonial-era barracks or multifamily housing units in favor of individual family dwellings. Planters typically set slave quarters a decent walking distance from the big house, which afforded slave families much-needed privacy, limited the spread of disease, and, for the benefit of both owners and slaves, promoted gender union and childbearing. The centerpiece of the slave community was the nuclear family, housed in a freestanding dwelling. A typical slave house was a single-story log construction measuring about 16 feet by 16 feet, with earthen floors, shuttered windows, a log chimney covered in clay, and a loft. Drafty in the winter and bug-infested in the summer, these sparsely furnished structures routinely housed families of more than 10 members. Porches, lean-to sheds, root cellars, and chicken coops were standard additions. On smaller farms, slaves generally lived in cramped quarters inside the owner's home or an outbuilding such as a barn.

Although many slave narratives include accounts of hunger and malnourishment, most slaves by the early nineteenth century received sufficient caloric intake from their bland rations of cornmeal, salt pork, and molasses. On average, slave owners allotted 1 pound of cornmeal and a half-pound of salt pork to each adult slave per day. In the Low Country and Louisiana, rice frequently replaced cornmeal as the grain of choice. While ample in calories, however, the basic diet of corn or rice and pork generally lacked or inhibited the utilization of essential vitamins and amino acids, compromising good nutrition. For the most part, however, inadequacies reflected the generally poor understanding of nutrition in the nineteenth century; most slave owners understood that willful starvation or malnourishment of their slaves would only cause a decline in value. Indeed, many slaves were allowed to plant their own kitchen gardens, which provided added nutrients in the form of sweet potatoes, peas, peppers, peanuts, and a variety of green, leafy vegetables. Some slaves were able to supplement protein intake through fishing and hunting.

With slave women typically cooking for their masters, African and European culinary traditions merged in the big-house kitchen to yield

Living conditions for slaves improved in the mid-nineteenth century but remained harsh. Slave cabins, often housing 10 or more, were cold in winter and bug-infested in summer.

masterpieces of evolving Southern cuisine. By means of slow cooking and the use of spicy condiments, slaves learned to turn tough cuts of meat, such as ribs, into delicacies. The African custom of one-pot meals combined common Southern ingredients into such regional favorites as hopping John (a mixture of rice, cowpeas, and salt pork or bacon); jambalaya (seasoned rice mixed with shrimp, chicken, or other kinds of meat); gumbo (a stew featuring okra, accompanied by other vegetables and meat); and pilau (a dish of rice and vegetables cooked in soup stock, sometimes with meat or fish). Evening supper was the big meal of the day, with the leftovers frequently serving as the next day's breakfast. Lunch, usually eaten in the midday heat, often consisted of makeshift corn bread, called hoecakes, baked literally on a hoe placed over a flame.

Southern slaves generally were not in a position to make the kinds of improvements to their clothing that they were to their food.

Except for domestic servants, masters provided slaves with clothes that were inexpensive and designed for practicality and durability rather than for comfort or appearance. By the late eighteenth century, adult slaves typically received a new set of clothes each spring and fall. Made of inexpensive, thin, rough "negro cloth," the set often would consist of two shirts and two pairs of trousers for men and two dresses for women, with a coat in winter. Discarded clothing from the big house sometimes made its way to the slave quarters, where it could be worn or turned into material for quilts. Women frequently wore head kerchiefs, both for protection from the sun and to perpetuate West African tradition. Shoes, produced on or off the plantation, were so uncomfortable and shoddily made that many slaves preferred to go barefoot. Slave children typically wore a shirttail—a one-piece, knee-length garment resembling a long shirt—until about the age of 12.

Discipline and Punishment

While physical abuse was anathema to the paternalistic ideal, slave owners claimed both the right and responsibility to exert all necessary control over their property and to impose corporal punishment as circumstances required. Paternalistic masters believed that slaves of any age were like small children, requiring physical correction to guide them on the path to dutiful obedience. But not all slave owners even understood or embraced the paternalistic ethic, and fewer still adhered to its restraints. Indeed many fell prey to their anger, frustration, paranoia, or lust, and on a frequent basis. There is simply no denying that violence, abuse, and intimidation—often unspeakably brutal—remained a central feature of slavery in America from beginning to end.

Masters and mistresses punished slaves for countless real or perceived misdeeds; lying, laziness, theft, insolence, and running away were commonly cited offenses. Whipping was a routine form of punishment; some masters preferred paddling or physical confinement. Owners and overseers typically administered corporal punishment in public to demonstrate the consequences of disobedience to other slaves. Although many slaves claimed never to have been whipped or beaten, most could recall having seen others subjected to physical punishment.

The prevalence of physical punishment was both a cause and consequence of slave resistance. The most severe form of defiance—organized revolt—struck particular fear in the hearts of slaveholders and was punishable by death. Indeed, any slave who raised his hand to a white person was subject to execution. Captured runaways faced a severe whipping and might be forced to wear a cumbersome iron collar with bells, to announce any further escape attempts. More subtle forms of slave resistance, recognized or not by their owners, included slow or poor workmanship, refusal to report on fellow slaves, theft, and arson.

Recreation and Religion

Slaves generally worked six days a week, with Sundays off; many worked only a half-day on Saturdays. Weekday evenings were devoted to domestic activities—tending a garden, hunting and fishing, preparing the evening meal, tending the children, mending clothes, and such. On weekends, some masters allowed their slaves to visit nearby towns to sell their produce or eggs.

Others granted passes on Saturday night that allowed slaves to visit a spouse, children, or friends on a nearby property. Weekends might also be an occasion for a slave dance or frolic, at which musicians and dancers could demonstrate their skills and young men and women could court.

Christian slaves often walked several miles to attend church on Sunday or an annual camp meeting organized by Baptists, Methodists, and Presbyterians. While some masters required their slaves to attend church, most allowed them simply to rest, play, or work for themselves on Sunday. Christian slaves who were prohibited from attending church or were dissatisfied with white religious services often conducted prayer meetings in their own quarters or slipped into the woods to worship as they saw fit. At Christmas, most slaves were given a week off from work and allowed to visit and celebrate with nearby friends and family.

Culture

A distinctive African American culture, according to historians, began to take shape prior to the American Revolution and reached maturity by the 1830s. While the culture found expression in diverse regional groups, such as the Gullah of the Low Country and the Creoles of Louisiana, it also reflected a broad confluence of African, European, and Native American traditions. Of these influences, of course, it was native African customs and folkways that most defined and characterized the North American slave culture.

From the beginning, African-born slaves had come from different tribes, spoke different languages, and practiced different customs. The fact that they were thrown together on the same plantations made it hard to preserve their cultural traditions and pass them on to future generations. Whites, who regarded African culture as uncivilized and a breeding ground of slave rebellion, sought to accelerate the process of cultural erosion by prohibiting the display of ancestral customs and by deterring or outlawing slave literacy. Nevertheless, significant elements of native African heritage managed to survive as part of an evolving African American culture through shared experience, interregional migration, and use of a common language (English).

By the early nineteenth century, North American slave quarters had become the incubator of a distinctive culture in which unique features came to life almost daily and, in doing so, revealed a persistent African influence. Drawing on African oral tradition, for example, slave elders entertained children and enlightened adults with folktales about wily tricksters who outsmarted the powerful with their wits. Craftsmen carved walking sticks or weaved baskets that reflected African iconography and design. Field hands indulged in line singing and call-and-response chanting, both rooted in African tradition (and forerunners of spiritual, gospel, and blues music). Many non-Christian slaves, like their African ancestors, also lived in a world in which contact with spirits was still considered the norm. Conjurers, male and female spirit workers who invoked native rituals and beliefs, assisted fellow slaves by offering charms and incantations to protect them from vengeful masters, shield them from haunts, cure disease, or attract a mate.

In all these ways and others, American slaves did their best to adapt to an oppressive and subservient way of life, maintain a sense of pride and identity, and forge cultural bonds between native ancestors and future generations.

Daniel L. Fountain and Jeff Hacker

See also: Abolitionist and Antislavery Movements

Sidelight

Rediscovering Early African American Fiction

While the slave prodigy Phillis Wheatley of Boston is widely recognized as the founder of the African American literary tradition for her celebrated *Poems on Various Subjects, Religious and Moral* (1773), the first book published by a black person in British North America, the pioneers of African American prose fiction have gone largely unrecognized for centuries. Even as the slave narrative emerged as a new and uniquely American literary genre during the antebellum period, by far the best-known fictional account of the slave experience was by a white woman, Harriet Beecher Stowe's *Uncle Tom's Cabin* (1852). In fact, it was not until 1982 that the novel now recognized as the first to be published by an African American—Harriet Wilson's *Our Nig* (1859)—came fully to light.

Most of what is known about Wilson and her novel has been pieced together by literary historians in recent decades. She was born Harriet E. Adams as a free person of color in Milford, New Hampshire, around 1825. After the death of her father when she was 6 and abandonment by her mother shortly thereafter, she became an indentured servant to the family of a wealthy Milford farmer named Nehemiah Hayward, Jr. Suffering through years of abuse, she remained bound as an indentured servant until age 18 and supported herself thereafter as a house servant and seamstress while coping with poverty, poor health, and an unsuccessful marriage to an abolitionist lecturer named Thomas Wilson.

Sometime in the mid-1850s, Harriet Wilson moved to Boston, where she raised a son in poverty and started writing a book to raise money. A fictional account based heavily on her own experiences, the novel was titled *Our Nig: Sketches from the Life of a Free Black: In a Two-Story White House, North: Showing That Slavery's Shadows Fall Even There*. The book was a kind of literary hybrid—a slavelike narrative in the form of a sentimental novel—that recounted the mistreatment of a mixed-race servant named Frado at the hands of a New England family named Bellmont. Written for a black audience, the account was intended to rally opposition to indentured servitude.

The Boston printing firm of George C. Rand and Avery issued the 132-page volume in modest quantity on September 5, 1859, whereupon *Our Nig* promptly fell into obscurity. Although it appeared at a time when abolitionist activism and the sale of antislavery books were at their height, Wilson's work faced several disadvantages. First, although the institution of indentured servitude was cruel and unjust, it did not resonate with Northern readers as much as the issue of slavery. In that regard, *Our Nig* was overshadowed by the earlier, and more gripping, *Uncle Tom's Cabin*. Perhaps above all, while liberal Northerners could accept African Americans as the authors of slave narratives, even they had difficulty embracing the notion of a black novelist.

After *Our Nig*, Wilson never wrote for publication again. She went on to lead an active life as a social reformer and lecturer, fighting for labor laws and educational reform. In the late 1860s, she became deeply involved in the Spiritualist movement, visiting local communities to address fellow believers and assist in contacting the spirits of the dead. She worked for many years as a nurse and as a housekeeper at a boardinghouse, before dying on June 28, 1900, in Quincy, Massachusetts.

Harriet Wilson and *Our Nig* remained virtually unknown until the early 1980s, when African American Studies scholar Henry Louis Gates, Jr., was browsing the shelves of a New York City rare-book store and pulled out a slim, fraying copy. Despite thinking that it was just another example of racist plantation literature by a white author, Gates purchased the book, began investigating, and documented enough information about the author to conclude that the work was in fact a fictionalized account. This made it the earliest published novel by an African American author yet discovered. Random House published a new edition in 1983, with an introduction by Gates. Said the acclaimed African American writer Alice Walker (author of

The Color Purple, 1982), Wilson's novel presents "a whole new layer of time and existence in American life and literature." Said Gates, "This poor woman Harriet Wilson is finally having her day."

Continuing his efforts to unearth the roots of African American literature, Gates made a new discovery in 2001—a manuscript said to supplant *Our Nig* as the first known novel written by a black person in the United States, albeit unpublished. Gates acquired the manuscript, titled *The Bondwoman's Narrative,* at auction in a New York antiquities house in 2001. As verified by subsequent research, the manuscript was written by a runaway house slave from North Carolina named Hannah Crafts who fictionalized events and characters from her own life. As in the case of *Our Nig,* Crafts produced a kind of slave narrative in the style of the sentimental novels that were popular at the time. According to historians, the manuscript may have been written as early as 1853, which would make it several years older than *Our Nig*. In any event, the first published edition of *The Bondwoman's Narrative* did not appear until 2002 and became a best seller.

Christopher Bates and Jeff Hacker

Stowe, Harriet Beecher

(1811–1896)

Author and activist Harriet Beecher Stowe is best known for her powerful antislavery novel *Uncle Tom's Cabin* (1852), an enormously popular work that gave millions of Americans their first view of the slave experience through the eyes of those in bondage. The book and stage adaptation changed the popular perception of slavery, energized the abolitionist movement, and pushed the nation closer to civil war.

She was born Harriet Elizabeth Beecher on June 14, 1811, in Litchfield, Connecticut. Her father, Lyman Beecher, was a renowned Presbyterian minister as well as an activist for the temperance and abolitionist causes. Her mother, Roxana Foote Beecher, died when Harriet was 5 years old. Many of the Beecher children achieved prominence, among them Harriet's sister Catharine Beecher, a noted educator; brothers Henry Ward Beecher and Charles Beecher, both Congregationalist ministers and social reformers active in the abolitionist movement; and sister Isabella Beecher Hooker, a leader in the woman suffrage movement. Harriet studied and later taught at Hartford Female Seminary, which was founded and operated by her sister Catharine. In 1832, her father accepted the presidency of Lane Theological Seminary, and the family moved to Cincinnati, Ohio. There, Harriet met and married Calvin Stowe, a minister and professor at Lane.

Six of the Stowes' seven children were born during their years in Cincinnati. It also was during this time that slavery became more than an abstract concept for the Beecher family. Although Lyman Beecher had preached against slavery throughout his career, living just across the Ohio River from the slave state of Kentucky gave Harriet and the rest of the family firsthand experience with the institution. The Beechers grew even more vocal in their opposition to slavery and became active in the Underground Railroad.

As her father and brothers attained prominence as clergymen and social activists, Harriet Beecher Stowe became frustrated because women of her era generally were discouraged from taking a role in public affairs. While she paid lip service to the gender role that was expected of her—"the nursery and the kitchen [are] my principal fields of labor," she once remarked—Stowe was a gifted intellectual and longed for engagement with society at large. "The bitterest tears shed over graves," she observed, "are for words left unsaid and deeds left undone." While in Cincinnati, she began attending meetings of the Semi-Colon Club, a social and literary society. She also took up her pen, contributing a number of articles to *Godey's Lady's Book.*

In 1850, the Stowes moved to Brunswick, Maine, where Calvin joined the faculty of Bowdoin College. Also that year, the U.S. Congress passed the Fugitive Slave Law, which required Northerners to assist in the capture of runaway slaves. Deeply disturbed by the implications of the law, both for slaves and for her fellow abolitionists, Stowe began work on a series of sketches about slavery that would become the novel *Uncle Tom's Cabin.* Although she had lived across the river from Kentucky for years, she had never actually visited the South and had to be creative in her research. She drew on her experience with black servants and read slave narratives and other published accounts of slavery. She also interviewed people who had lived and traveled in the South.

Uncle Tom's Cabin first appeared in weekly installments in the abolitionist periodical *The National Era,* starting in June 1851. Stowe's narrative tells the story of the heroic and long-suffering slave Uncle Tom, who perseveres through a series of tragedies before being killed at the hands of evil plantation owner Simon Legree. Highly popular in serial form, the story was published the following year as a two-volume novel titled *Uncle Tom's Cabin; or, Life Among the Lowly.* Packed with vivid details, the book was an attack not only on slavery but also on the complicity of church officials in perpetuating the institution and on the indifference of the Northern public.

The novel was translated into more than 60 languages and became an international best seller; only the Bible sold more copies in nineteenth-century America. *Uncle Tom's Cabin* also was adapted into a popular play that toured the country. Its in-

Harriet Beecher Stowe, the daughter of famed minister and abolitionist Lyman Beecher, gained a firsthand view of slave life while living in Cincinnati, across the river from Kentucky.

fluence on antebellum America was so great that, according to legend, when President Abraham Lincoln met Stowe in 1862, he exclaimed, "So this is the little woman who wrote the book that started this Great War!"

Not everyone embraced her work, of course. Supporters of slavery vehemently attacked Stowe in the press and in a spate of proslavery "anti-Tom" novels. She was so affected by the criticisms that in 1853 she published *A Key to Uncle Tom's Cabin,* a nonfiction work that attempted to demonstrate the veracity of her claims.

Uncle Tom's Cabin made Stowe a celebrity and launched a long writing career in which she published 30 books and numerous shorter pieces. Also prominent among her works are another antislavery novel, *Dred* (1856), as well as *The Minister's Wooing* (1859), *The Pearl of Orr Island* (1862), and *Old Town Folks* (1869). All were best sellers and received favorable reviews, but none came close to matching the success of *Uncle Tom's Cabin*.

In 1864, upon Calvin's retirement, the Stowes relocated to Hartford, Connecticut, where they would become neighbors of an up-and-coming Samuel Clemens (a.k.a. Mark Twain). The Stowes remained in Hartford for the rest of their lives. Harriet died there on July 1, 1896.

Harriet Beecher Stowe's reputation as a writer declined precipitously in the decades after her death. Her novels were dismissed by many as maudlin and melodramatic, epitomizing the sentimental literature of the day. More significantly, she was roundly criticized for the African American stereotypes perpetuated by *Uncle Tom's Cabin:* the mammy, the unkempt and wild-eyed slave child, and the docile Uncle Tom. While such stereotypes were based in large part on Stowe's characters, they were exaggerated and twisted in the novel's many adaptations, especially stage satires and postwar minstrel shows. Indeed, the figures of "Uncle Tom" and "Topsy" that became icons of American racism were much changed from their namesakes in *Uncle Tom's Cabin*.

Contemporary scholars and readers, following a resurgence of interest in both women's literature and the sentimental culture dismissed by earlier critics, have rediscovered Stowe's work and its literary merits. *Uncle Tom's Cabin* gained new recognition for its social and political realism, which broke new ground in American fiction. Although debate persists over Stowe's portrayal of black Americans, she has become a focal point of scholarship and critical analysis in nineteenth-century American history and literature. Whatever one's critical perspective, the impact of her novel on the debate over slavery, on nineteenth-century American culture, and on the future of social protest literature in America cannot be denied.

Ryan C. Cordell

See also: Abolitionist and Antislavery Movements; Slavery and Slave Life

Chapter 45, "Concluding Remarks," *Uncle Tom's Cabin*, 1852

Few if any other works in the American literary canon have had a more momentous effect on national affairs than Harriet Beecher Stowe's Uncle Tom's Cabin; or, Life Among the Lowly. *In response to the Fugitive Slave Law of 1850, Stowe sought to rouse the conscience of the nation by capitalizing on the popular taste for melodrama with a fictional—if brutally realistic—tale that laid bare all the worst aspects of slavery. The effort succeeded. After appearing in 40 weekly journal installments,* Uncle Tom's Cabin *was published as a novel in 1852 and sold 300,000 copies in the first year. It became the most discussed and influential document of the American antislavery movement. In the final chapter, reproduced here, Stowe discusses the line between fiction and reality, and delivers a kind of antislavery sermon to readers.*

The writer has often been inquired of, by correspondents from different parts of the country, whether this narrative is a true one; and to these inquiries she will give one general answer.

The separate incidents that compose the narrative are, to a very great extent, authentic, occurring, many of them, either under her own observation, or that of her personal friends. She or her friends have observed characters the counterpart of almost all that are here introduced; and many of the sayings are word for word as heard herself, or reported to her.

The personal appearance of Eliza, the character ascribed to her, are sketches drawn from life. The incorruptible fidelity, piety and honesty, of Uncle Tom, had more than one development, to her personal knowledge. Some of the most deeply tragic and romantic, some of the most terrible incidents, have also their parallels in reality. The incident of the mother's crossing the Ohio river on the ice is a well-known fact. The story of "old Prue," in the second volume, was an incident that fell under the personal observation of a brother of the writer, then collecting-clerk to a large mercantile house, in New Orleans. From the same source was derived the character of the planter Legree. Of him her brother thus wrote, speaking of visiting his plantation, on a collecting tour; "He actually made me feel of his fist, which was like a blacksmith's hammer, or a nodule of iron, telling me that it was 'calloused with knocking down niggers.' When I left the plantation, I drew a long breath, and felt as if I had escaped from an ogre's den."

That the tragical fate of Tom, also, has too many times had its parallel, there are living witnesses, all over our land, to testify. Let it be remembered that in all southern states it is a principle of jurisprudence that no person of colored lineage can testify in a suit against a white, and it will be easy to see that such a case may occur, wherever there is a man whose passions outweigh his interests, and a slave who has manhood or principle enough to resist his will. There is, actually, nothing to protect the slave's life, but the *character* of the master. Facts too shocking to be contemplated occasionally force their way to the public ear, and the comment that one often hears made on them is more shocking than the thing itself. It is said, "Very likely such cases may now and then occur, but they are no sample of general practice." If the laws of New England were so arranged that a master could *now and then* torture an apprentice to death, would it be received with equal composure? Would it be said, "These cases are rare, and no samples of general practice"? This injustice is an *inherent* one in the slave system,—it cannot exist without it.

The public and shameless sale of beautiful mulatto and quadroon girls has acquired a notoriety, from the incidents following the capture of the Pearl. We extract the following from the speech of Hon. Horace Mann, one of the legal counsel for the defendants in that case. He says: "In that company of seventy-six persons, who attempted, in 1848, to escape from the District of Columbia in the schooner Pearl, and whose officers I assisted in defending, there were several young and healthy girls, who had those peculiar attractions of form and feature which connoisseurs prize so highly. Elizabeth Russel was one of them. She immediately fell into the slave-trader's fangs, and was doomed for the New Orleans market. The hearts of those that saw her were touched with pity for her fate. They offered eighteen hundred dollars to redeem her; and some there were who offered to give, that would not have much left after the gift; but the fiend of a slave-trader was inexorable. She was despatched to New Orleans; but, when about half way there, God had mercy on her, and smote her with death. There were two girls named Edmundson in the same company. When about to be sent to the same market, an older sister went to the shambles, to plead with the wretch who owned them, for the love of God, to spare his victims. He bantered her, telling what fine dresses and fine furniture they would have. 'Yes,' she said, 'that may do very well in this life, but what will become of them in the next?' They too were sent to New Orleans; but were afterwards redeemed, at an enormous ransom, and brought back." Is it not plain, from this, that the histories of Emmeline and Cassy may have many counterparts?

Justice, too, obliges the author to state that the fairness of mind and generosity attributed to St. Clare are not without a parallel, as the following anecdote will show. A few years since, a young southern gentleman was in Cincinnati, with a favorite servant, who had been his personal attendant from a boy. The young man took advantage of this opportunity to secure his own freedom, and fled to the protection of a Quaker, who was quite noted in affairs of this kind. The owner was exceedingly indignant. He had always treated the slave with such indulgence, and his confidence in his affection was such, that he believed he must have been practised upon to induce him to revolt from him. He visited the Quaker, in high anger; but, being possessed of uncommon candor and fairness, was soon quieted by his arguments and representations. It was a side of the subject which he never had heard,—never had thought on; and he immediately told the Quaker that, if his slave would, to his own face, say that it was his desire to be free, he would liberate him. An interview was forthwith procured, and Nathan was asked by his young master whether he had ever had any reason to complain of his treatment, in any respect.

"No, Mas'r," said Nathan; "you've always been good to me."

"Well, then, why do you want to leave me?"

"Mas'r may die, and then who get me?—I'd rather be a free man."

After some deliberation, the young master replied, "Nathan, in your place, I think I should feel very much so, myself. You are free."

He immediately made him out free papers; deposited a sum of money in the hands of the Quaker, to be judiciously used in assisting him to start in life, and left a very sensible and kind letter of advice to the young man. That letter was for some time in the writer's hands.

The author hopes she has done justice to that nobility, generosity, and humanity, which in many cases characterize individuals at the South. Such instances save us from utter despair of our kind. But, she asks any person, who knows the world, are such characters *common,* anywhere?

For many years of her life, the author avoided all reading upon or allusion to the subject of slavery, considering it as too painful to be inquired into, and one which advancing light and civilization would certainly live down. But, since the legislative act of 1850, when she heard, with perfect surprise and consternation, Christian and humane people actually recommending the remanding escaped fugitives into slavery, as a duty binding on good citizens,—when she heard, on all hands, from kind, compassionate and estimable people, in the free states of the North, deliberations and discussions as to what Christian duty could be on this head,—she could only think, These men and Christians cannot know what slavery is; if they did, such a question could never be open for discussion. And from this arose a desire to exhibit it in a *living dramatic reality.* She has endeavored to show it fairly, in its best and its worst phases. In its *best* aspect, she has, perhaps, been successful; but, oh! who shall say what yet remains untold in that valley and shadow of death, that lies the other side?

To you, generous, noble-minded men and women, of the South,—you, whose virtue, and magnanimity and purity of character, are the greater for the severer trial it has encountered,—to you is her appeal. Have you not, in your own secret souls, in your own private conversings, felt that there are woes and evils, in this accursed system, far beyond what are here shadowed, or can be shadowed? Can it be otherwise? Is *man* ever a creature to be trusted with wholly irresponsible power? And does not the slave system, by denying the slave all legal right of testimony, make every individual owner an irresponsible despot? Can anybody fail to make the inference what the practical result will be? If there is, as we admit, a public sentiment among you, men of honor, justice and humanity, is there not also another kind of public sentiment among the ruffian, the brutal and debased? And cannot the ruffian, the brutal, the debased, by slave law, own just as many slaves as the best and purest? Are the honorable, the just, the high-minded and compassionate, the majority anywhere in this world?

The writer has given only a faint shadow, a dim picture, of the anguish and despair that are ... riving thousands of hearts, shattering thousands of families.

The slave-trade is now, by American law, considered as piracy. But a slave-trade, as systematic as ever was carried on on the coast of Africa, is an inevitable attendant and result of American slavery. And its heart-break and its horrors, can they be told?

The writer has given only a faint shadow, a dim picture, of the anguish and despair that are, at this very moment, riving thousands of hearts, shattering thousands of families, and driving a helpless and sensitive race to frenzy and despair. There are those living who know the mothers whom this accursed traffic has driven to the murder of their children; and themselves seeking in death a shelter from woes more dreaded than death. Nothing of tragedy can be written, can be spoken, can be conceived, that equals the frightful reality of scenes daily and hourly acting on our shores, beneath the shadow of American law, and the shadow of the cross of Christ.

And now, men and women of America, is this a thing to be trifled with, apologized for, and passed over in silence? Farmers of Massachusetts, of New Hampshire, of Vermont, of Connecticut, who read this book by the blaze of your winter-evening fire,—strong-hearted, generous sailors and ship-owners of Maine,—is this a thing for you to countenance and encourage? Brave and generous men of New York, farmers of rich and joyous Ohio, and ye of the wide prairie states,—answer, is this a thing for you to protect and countenance? And you, mothers of America,—you who have learned, by the cradles of your own children, to love and feel for all mankind,—by the sacred love you bear your child; by your joy in his beautiful, spotless infancy; by the motherly pity and tenderness with which you guide his growing years; by the anxieties of his education; by the prayers you breathe for his soul's eternal good;—I beseech you, pity the mother who has all your affections, and not one legal right to protect, guide, or educate, the child of her bosom! By the sick hour of your child; by those dying eyes, which you can never forget; by those last cries, that wrung your heart when you could neither help nor save; by the desolation of that empty cradle, that silent nursery,—I beseech you, pity those mothers that are constantly made childless by the American slave-trade! And say, mothers of America, is this a thing to be defended, sympathized with, passed over in silence?

Do you say that the people of the free state have nothing to do with it, and can do nothing? Would to God this were true! But it is not true. The people of the free states have defended, encouraged, and participated; and are more guilty for it, before God, than the South, in that they have not the apology of education or custom.

If the mothers of the free states had all felt as they should, in times past, the sons of the free states would not have been the holders, and, proverbially, the hardest masters of slaves; the sons of the free states would not have connived at the extension of slavery, in our national body; the sons of the free states would not, as they do, trade the souls and bodies of men as an equivalent to money, in their mercantile dealings. There are multitudes of slaves temporarily owned, and sold again, by merchants in northern cities; and shall the whole guilt or obloquy of slavery fall only on the South?

Northern men, northern mothers, northern Christians, have something more to do than denounce their brethren at the South; they have to look to the evil among themselves.

But, what can any individual do? Of that, every individual can judge. There is one thing that every individual can do,—they can see to it that *they feel right.* An atmosphere of sympathetic influence encircles every human being; and the man or woman who *feels* strongly, healthily and justly, on the great interests of humanity, is a constant benefactor to the human race. See, then, to your sympathies in this matter! Are they in harmony with the sympathies of Christ? or are they swayed and perverted by the sophistries of worldly policy?

Christian men and women of the North! still further,—you have another power; you can *pray!* Do you believe in prayer? or has it become an indistinct apostolic tradition? You pray for the heathen abroad; pray also for the heathen at home. And pray for those distressed Christians whose whole chance of religious improvement is an accident of trade and sale; from whom any adherence to the morals of Christianity is, in many cases, an impossibility, unless they have given them, from above, the courage and grace of martyrdom.

But, still more. On the shores of our free states are emerging the poor, shattered, broken remnants of families,—men and women, escaped, by miraculous providences from the surges of slavery,—feeble in knowledge, and, in many cases, infirm in moral constitution, from a system which confounds and confuses every principle of Christianity and morality. They come to seek a refuge among you; they come to seek education, knowledge, Christianity.

What do you owe to these poor unfortunates, oh Christians? Does not every American Christian owe to the African race some effort at reparation for the wrongs that the American nation has brought upon them? Shall the doors of churches and school-houses be shut upon them? Shall states arise and shake them out? Shall the church of Christ hear in silence the taunt that is thrown at them, and shrink away from the helpless hand that they stretch out; and, by her silence, encourage the cruelty that would chase them from our borders? If it must be so, it will be a mournful spectacle. If it must be so, the country will have reason to tremble, when it remembers that the fate of nations is in the hands of One who is very pitiful, and of tender compassion.

Do you say, "We don't want them here; let them go to Africa"?

That the providence of God has provided a refuge in Africa, is, indeed, a great and noticeable fact; but that is no reason why the church of Christ should throw off that responsibility to this outcast race which her profession demands of her.

To fill up Liberia with an ignorant, inexperienced, half-barbarized race, just escaped from the chains of slavery, would be only to prolong, for ages, the period of struggle and conflict which attends the inception of new enterprises. Let the church of the north receive these poor sufferers in the spirit of Christ; receive them to the educating advantages of Christian republican society and schools, until they have attained to somewhat of a moral and intellectual maturity, and then assist them in their passage to those shores, where they may put in practice the lessons they have learned in America.

There is a body of men at the north, comparatively small, who have been doing this; and, as the result, this country has already seen examples of men, formerly slaves, who have rapidly acquired property, reputation, and education. Talent has been developed, which, considering the circumstances, is certainly remarkable; and, for moral traits of honesty, kindness, tenderness of feeling,—for heroic efforts and self-denials, endured for the ransom of brethren and friends yet in slavery,—they have been remarkable to a degree that, considering the influence under which they were born, is surprising.

The writer has lived, for many years, on the frontier-line of slave states, and has had great opportunities of observation among those who formerly were slaves. They have been in her family as servants; and, in default of any other school to receive them, she has, in many cases, had them instructed in a family school, with her own children. She has also the testimony of missionaries, among the fugitives in Canada, in coincidence with her own experience; and her deductions, with regard to the capabilities of the race, are encouraging in the highest degree.

The first desire of the emancipated slave, generally, is for *education.* There is nothing that they are not willing to give or do to have their children instructed, and, so far as the writer has observed herself, or taken the testimony of teachers among them, they are remarkably intelligent and quick to learn. The results of schools, founded for them by benevolent individuals in Cincinnati, fully establish this.

The author gives the following statement of facts, on the authority of Professor C. E. Stowe, then of Lane Seminary, Ohio, with regard to emancipated slaves, now resident in Cincinnati; given to show the capability of the race, even without any very particular assistance or encouragement.

The initial letters alone are given. They are all residents of Cincinnati.

"B——. Furniture maker; twenty years in the city; worth ten thousand dollars, all his own earnings; a Baptist.

"C——. Full black; stolen from Africa; sold in New Orleans; been free fifteen years; paid for himself six hundred dollars; a farmer; owns several farms in Indiana; Presbyterian; probably worth fifteen or twenty thousand dollars, all earned by himself.

"K——. Full black; dealer in real estate; worth thirty thousand dollars; about forty years old; free six years; paid eighteen hundred dollars for his family; member of the Baptist church; received a legacy from his master, which he has taken good care of, and increased.

"G——. Full black; coal dealer; about thirty years old; worth eighteen thousand dollars; paid for himself twice, being once defrauded to the amount of sixteen hundred dollars; made all his money by his own efforts—much of it while a slave, hiring his time of his master, and doing business for himself; a fine, gentlemanly fellow.

"W——. Three-fourths black; barber and waiter; from Kentucky; nineteen years free; paid for self and family over three thousand dollars; deacon in the Baptist church.

"G. D——. Three-fourths black; white-washer; from Kentucky; nine years free; paid fifteen hundred dollars for self and family; recently died, aged sixty; worth six thousand dollars."

Professor Stowe says, "With all these, except G——, I have been, for some years, personally acquainted, and make my statements from my own knowledge."

The writer well remembers an aged colored woman, who was employed as a washerwoman in her father's family. The daughter of this woman married a slave. She was a remarkably active and capable young woman, and, by her industry and thrift, and the most persevering self-denial, raised nine hundred dollars for her husband's freedom, which she paid, as she raised it, into the hands of his master. She yet wanted a hundred dollars of the price, when he died. She never recovered any of the money.

These are but few facts, among multitudes which might be adduced, to show the self-denial, energy, patience, and honesty, which the slave has exhibited in a state of freedom.

And let it be remembered that these individuals have thus bravely succeeded in conquering for themselves comparative wealth and social position, in the face of every disadvantage and discouragement. The colored man, by the law of Ohio, cannot be a voter, and, till within a few years, was even denied the right of testimony in legal suits with the white. Nor are these instances confined to the State of Ohio. In all states of the Union we see men, but yesterday burst from the shackles of slavery, who, by a self-educating force, which cannot be too much admired, have risen to highly respectable stations in society. Pennington, among clergymen, Douglas and Ward, among editors, are well known instances.

If this persecuted race, with every discouragement and disadvantage, have done thus much, how much more they might do if the Christian church would act towards them in the spirit of her Lord!

This is an age of the world when nations are trembling and convulsed. A mighty influence is abroad, surging and heaving the world, as with an earthquake. And is America safe? Every nation that carries in its bosom great and unredressed injustice has in it the elements of this last convulsion.

For what is this mighty influence thus rousing in all nations and languages those groanings that cannot be uttered, for man's freedom and equality?

O, Church of Christ, read the signs of the times! Is not this power the spirit of Him whose kingdom is yet to come, and whose will to be done on earth as it is in heaven?

But who may abide the day of his appearing? "for that day shall burn as an oven: and he shall appear as a swift witness against those that oppress the hireling in his wages, the widow and the fatherless, and that *turn aside the stranger in his right:* and he shall break in pieces the oppressor."

Are not these dread words for a nation bearing in her bosom so mighty an injustice? Christians! every time that you pray that the kingdom of Christ may come, can you forget that prophecy associates, in dread fellowship, the *day of vengeance* with the year of his redeemed?

A day of grace is yet held out to us. Both North and South have been guilty before God; and the *Christian church* has a heavy account to answer. Not by combining together, to protect injustice and cruelty, and making a common capital of sin, is this Union to be saved,—but by repentance, justice and mercy; for, not surer is the eternal law by which the millstone sinks in the ocean, than that stronger law, by which injustice and cruelty shall bring on nations the wrath of Almighty God!

Source: Harriet Beecher Stowe, *Uncle Tom's Cabin; or, Life Among the Lowly* (Boston: John P. Jewett & Company, 1852).

Underground Railroad

The Underground Railroad was a clandestine, loosely organized network of routes and hiding places operated by free African Americans and white abolitionists with the purpose of guiding runaway slaves to freedom in the Northern states or Canada. The vast network was not run by a single individual or organization but was a highly effective system that involved the efforts of thousands of opponents of slavery by the 1850s. From 1820 to 1860, an estimated 30,000–100,000 African American slaves used "the only free road," as Henry David Thoreau described it, to reach freedom.

The first antislavery activists in North America came from religious groups, most prominently the Quakers. Aiding runaway African American slaves as early as the 1680s, the Quakers organized their efforts with increasing zeal and efficiency over the course of the next century and beyond. In 1786, George Washington himself complained that one of his fugitive slaves had been aided by a group of Quakers expressly mobilized to assist runaway slaves. Members of the faith resisted the institution in other ways as well. In 1775, for example, Quaker leaders founded the Society for the Relief of Free Negroes Unlawfully Held in Bondage to campaign for the abolition of slavery through appeals to the Constitutional Convention and U.S. Congress, speeches, publications, and other means.

By the beginning of the nineteenth century, antislavery sentiment had moved beyond religious groups to include a growing cadre of secular leaders, intellectuals, philanthropists, and free African Americans. Many of the new converts had been alienated by political developments, especially the Fugitive Slave Law of 1793 and the Missouri Compromise of 1820. Others were inspired by the religious sentiment that swept the country during the Second Great Awakening in the first decades of the nineteenth century. In any event, by the

1820s, the growing hostility in the North to slavery had persuaded many white abolitionists, freed African American slaves, and Native Americans to follow the Quakers' example and form their own freedom networks.

Consistent with its decentralized nature, the Underground Railroad was nameless for much of its existence. In 1842, however, an article in the *New York Semi-Weekly Express* referred to the escape of slaves via an "underground railroad," and the phrase quickly gained popularity. Abolitionists, slaveholders, and participants all began adopting railroad parlance for various aspects of the network. The routes to freedom, which ran across 14 Northern states and Canada, were called "lines." Hiding places where the fugitives could rest and eat were referred to as "stations" or "depots," run by "stationmasters." Runaway slaves were called "passengers" and were guided to freedom by "conductors." Individuals who donated money to the network were "stockholders."

Finding the way to freedom was not an easy task for travelers on the Underground Railroad. Most had to plot their own escapes and make their own way to the first stop. Once in the hands of conductors, the passengers' outlook improved, but the journey was still difficult. Runaways typically traveled 10–20 miles at a time, almost always at night. Even when they reached their final destinations in the North, many escapees felt insecure because the Fugitive Slave Laws of 1793 and 1850 allowed magistrates and slave catchers to seize runaways in the Northern states and return them to their former masters. Fear of recapture prompted at least 20,000 fugitive slaves to move to Canada, referred to as "heaven" or the "promised land" in railroad parlance.

Serving as a conductor on the railroad presented enormous risks and difficulties as well, since it was a federal crime to assist slaves in the flight to freedom. Consequently, the operators of the railroad maintained strict security. Messages between conductors were communicated in code—for example, the arrival of four adult passengers and two children might be referred to as the "delivery of four large and two small hams." Historians have suggested that quilts hung on porches and clotheslines included designs that directed runaways to the next stop or that warned of danger, while the lyrics to spirituals and other songs likewise contained coded information about routes, stations, and other logistics. Participants in the Underground

In one of the most resourceful and audacious of all slave escapes, Henry "Box" Brown had himself shipped in a wooden produce crate from Richmond to Philadelphia.

Railroad operated in relative autonomy, often aware only of the conductors with whom they had direct contact. This helped protect participants, who could not be compelled to betray the names and locations of other conductors they did not know.

Despite grave risks, the Underground Railroad rarely suffered for a lack of willing volunteers, some of whom became famous for their exploits. In Indiana and Ohio, for example, Levi Coffin helped as many as 2,000 slaves escape to freedom and became known as the "President of the Underground Railroad." Former fugitive slave Harriet Tubman made at least 19 trips to the South during the 1850s and guided more than 300 slaves to freedom. Nicknamed "Moses" by grateful African Americans, she was justifiably proud of her record. "I was the conductor of the Underground Railroad for eight years," she later wrote, "and I can say what most conductors can't say—I never ran my train off the track and I never lost a passenger."

The Underground Railroad survived until the end of the Civil War and the abolition of slavery by the Thirteenth Amendment, both in

1865. It left behind a great legacy. In addition to all the slaves the network spirited away to freedom, its very existence helped push the slavery issue to the center of national politics. As such, it helped precipitate the Civil War and the ultimate end of slavery. After the war, along with prominent conductors such as Tubman, the Underground Railroad served as an important symbol of freedom for all Americans—especially members of the African American community.

Chris Kostov

See also: Abolitionist and Antislavery Movements; Slavery and Slave Life

Narrative of the Life of Henry Box Brown (excerpt), 1849

Of the many escape adventures in the annals of the Underground Railroad, few are as compelling as that of Virginia slave Henry "Box" Brown. Certainly none better illustrates the desperation and ingenuity of those held in bondage to gain their freedom. In 1848, despondent after the sale of his wife and children at auction, Brown arranged with a storekeeper in nearby Richmond to ship him inside a crate to Philadelphia, where he would be received by another operator of the Underground Railroad. Amazingly, the plan worked. After a 27-hour journey, part of which he spent upside down, Brown arrived at his destination safe and free. He became a prominent figure on the abolitionist speaking circuit and published a popular memoir. In the excerpt below, Brown recounts his remarkable adventure from the first idea to the opening of the crate in Philadelphia.

> One day, while I was at work, and my thoughts were eagerly feasting upon the idea of freedom, I felt my soul called out to heaven to breathe a prayer to Almighty God. I prayed fervently that he who seeth in secret and knew the inmost desires of my heart, would lend me his aid in bursting my fetters asunder, and in restoring me to the posession of those rights, of which men

had robbed me; when the idea suddenly flashed across my mind of shutting myself up in a box, and getting myself conveyed as dry goods to a free state.

Being now satisfied that this was the plan for me, I went to my friend Dr. Smith and, having aquainted him with it, we agreed to have it put at once into execution not however without calculating the chances of danger with which it was attended; but buoyed up by the prospect of freedom and increased hatred to slavery I was willing to dare even death itself rather than endure any longer the clanking of those galling chains[.] It being still necessary to have the assistance of the store-keeper, to see that the box was kept in its right position on its passage, I then went to let him know my intention, but he said although he was willing to serve me in any way he could, he did not think I could live in a box for so long a time as would be necessary to convey me to Philadelphia, but as I had already made up my mind, he consented to accompany me and keep the box right all the way.

My next object was to procure a box, and with the assistance of a carpenter that was very soon accomplished, and taken to the place where the packing was to be performed. In the mean time the storekeeper had written to a friend in Philadelphia, but as no answer had arrived, we resolved to carry out our purpose as best we could. It was deemed necessary that I should get permission to be absent from my work for a few days, in order to keep down suspicion until I had once fairly started on the road to liberty; and as I had then a gathered finger I thought that would form a very good excuse for obtaining leave of absence; but when I showed it to one everseer, Mr. Allen, he told me it was not so bad as to prevent me from working, so with a view of making it bad enough, I got Dr. Smith to procure for me some oil of vitriol in order to drop a little of this on it, but in my hurry I dropped rather much and made it worse than there was any *occasion for, in f*act it was very soon eaten in to the bone, and on presenting it again to Mr. Allen I obtained the permission required, with the advice that I should go home and get a poultice of flax-meal to it, and keep it well poulticed until it got better. I took him instantly at his word and went off directly to the store-keeper who had by this time received an answer from his friend in Philadelphia, and had obtained permission to address the box to him, this friend in that city, arranging to call for it as soon as it should arrive. There being no time to be lost, the store-keeper, Dr. Smith, and myself, agreed to meet next morning at four o'clock, in order to get the box ready for the express train. The box which I had procured was three feet one inch wide, two feet six inches high, and two feet wide: and on the morning of the 29th day of March, 1849, I went into the box—having previously bored three gimlet holes opposite my face, for air, and provided myself with a bladder of water, both for the purpose of quenching my thirst and for wetting my face, should I feel getting faint. I took the gimlet also with me, in order that I might bore more holes if I found I had not sufficient air. Being thus equipped for the battle of liberty, my friends nailed down the lid and had me conveyed to the Express Office, which was about a mile distant from the place where I was packed. I had no sooner arrived at the office than I was turned heels up, while some person nailed something on the end of the box. I was then put upon a waggon and driven off to the depôt with my head down, and I had no sooner arrived at the depôt, than the man who drove the waggon tumbled me roughly into the baggage car, where, however, I happened to fall on my right side.

Being thus equipped for the battle of liberty, my friends nailed down the lid and had me conveyed to the Express Office.

The next place we arrived at was Potomac Creek, where the baggage had to be removed from the cars, to be put on board the steamer; where I was again placed with my head down, and in this dreadful position had to remain nearly an hour and a half, which, from the sufferings I had thus to endure, seemed like an age to me, but I was forgetting the battle of liberty, and I was resolved to conquer or die. I felt my eyes swelling as if they would burst from their sockets; and the veins on my temples were dreadfully distended with pressure of blood upon my head. In this position I attempted to lift my hand to my face but I had no power to move it; I felt a cold sweat coming over me which seemed to be a warning that death was about to terminate my earthly miseries, but as I feared even that, less than slavery, I resolved to submit to the will of God, and under the influence of that impression, I lifted up my soul in prayer to God, who alone, was able to deliver me. My cry was soon heard, for I could hear a man saying to another, that he had travelled a long way and had been standing there two hours, and he would like to get somewhat to sit down; so perceiving my box, standing on end, he threw it down and then two sat upon it. I was thus relieved from a state of agony which may be more easily imagined than described[.] I could now listen to the men talking, and heard one of them asking the other what he supposed the box contained; his companion replied he guessed it was "THE MAIL." I too thought it was a mail but not such a mail as he supposed it to be.

The next place at which we arrived was the city of Washington, where I was taken from the steam-boat, and again placed upon a waggon and carried to the depôt right side up with care; but when the driver arrived at the depôt I heard him call for some person to help to take the box off the waggon, and some one answered him to the effect that he might throw it off; but, says the driver, it is marked "this side up with care;" so if I throw it off I might break something, the other answered him that it did not matter if he broke all that was in it, the railway company were able enough to pay for it. No sooner were these words spoken than I began to tumble from the waggon, and falling on the end where my head was, I could bear my neck give a crack, as if it had been snapped asunder and I was knocked completely insensible. The first thing I heard after that, was some person saying, "there is no room for the box, it will have to remain and be sent through to-morrow with the luggage train; but the Lord had not quite forsaken me, for in answer to my earnest prayer He so ordered affairs that I should not be left behind; and I now heard a man say that the box had come with the express, and it must be sent on. I was then tumbled into the car with my head downwards again, but the car had not proceeded far before, more luggage having to be taken in, my box got shifted about and so happened to turn upon its right side; and in this position I remained till I got to Philadelphia, of our arrival in which place

I was informed by hearing some person say, "We are in port and at Philadelphia." My heart then leaped for joy, and I wondered if any person knew that such a box was there.

Here it may be proper to observe that the man who had promised to accompany my box failed to do what he promised; but, to prevent it remaining long at the station after its arrival, he sent a telegraphic message to his friend, and I was only twenty seven hours in the box, though travelling a distance of three hundred and fifty miles.

I was now placed in the depôt amongst the other luggage, where I lay till seven o'clock, P.M., at which time a waggon drove up, and I heard a person inquire for such a box as that in which I was. I was then placed on a waggon and conveyed to the house where my friend in Richmond had arranged I should be received. A number of persons soon collected round the box after it was taken in to the house, but as I did not know what was going on I kept myself quiet. I heard a man say, "let us rap upon the box and see if he is alive;" and immediately a rap ensued and a voice said, tremblingly, "Is all right within?" to which I replied—"all right." *The joy of the friends was very* great; when they heard that I was alive they soon managed to break open the box, and then came my resurrection from the grave of slavery. I rose a freeman, but I was too weak, by reason of long confinement in that box, to be able to stand, so I immediately swooned away. After my recovery from the swoon the first thing, which arrested my attention, was the presence of a number of friends, every one seeming more anxious than another, to have an opportunity of rendering me their assistance, and of bidding me a hearty welcome to the possession of my natural rights, I had risen as it were from the dead. . . .

Sources: Documenting the American South, University of North Carolina at Chapel Hill (http://docsouth.unc.edu); *Henry Box Brown, Narrative of the Life of Henry Box Brown, Written by Himself* (Manchester, UK: Lee and Glynn, 1851).

Whitman, Walt

(1819–1892)

With Emily Dickinson, Walt Whitman is regarded as one of the two most acclaimed and influential American poets of the nineteenth century. During his lifetime, he was also one of the most controversial. His free-verse collection *Leaves of Grass,* published in 1855 and reissued in eight revised and expanded editions until his death, abandoned literary convention and broke cultural barriers in forging a distinctive national idiom of and for the "American masses." If relatively uncelebrated until late in his life, *Leaves of Grass* would come to be regarded as a literary masterpiece, revolutionizing American poetry and profoundly influencing readers and poets around the world. Its author came to be called the "father of free verse" and America's "poet of democracy."

Early Life and Work

The son of a Quaker carpenter, Walter Whitman was born on May 31, 1819, on Long Island, New York. Growing up among the working class in the town of Huntington, he ended his formal education by age 11 due to the family's financial straits, but remained an omnivorous reader. In 1830, with the family now living in Brooklyn, he went to work for two lawyers on Fulton Street. From their library shelves, he devoured copies of the *Arabian Nights* and works by Sir Walter Scott and James Fenimore Cooper.

Shortly thereafter, Whitman began apprenticing as a typesetter and printer at the *Long Island Patriot* and then the *Long-Island Star,* for which he also began writing filler pieces. In his early teens, he submitted verse to the *New York Mirror* and spent free evenings at the theater. In May 1835, at age 16, he left the *Star* and Brooklyn, moved to Manhattan, and found work as a compositor. The following spring, he rejoined his family on Long Island and taught school until 1838, when he resumed his newspaper career. He spent the next 10 years as a printer, writer, and editor for papers in the New York area, culminating in the editorship of the *Brooklyn Daily Eagle* in (1846–1848), then the city's leading daily.

Whitman lost his job at the *Eagle* in a political dispute with the paper's owner, Isaac Van Anden, over slavery. Whitman was a member of the free-soil wing of the state's Democratic Party, Anden a member of the more traditional wing, which downplayed the issue of slavery. In August 1848, Whitman served as a delegate to the first convention of the Free Soil Party in Buffalo, New York. Also that year, as a contributor to the *New Orleans Crescent*, he made an extended trip to the South, where he witnessed slavery firsthand, experienced the music and nightlife of the French Quarter, and found inspiration in the Mississippi River.

America's Poet

Upon returning to New York in 1849, Whitman eschewed conventional employment to pursue his craft as a poet. The following year, experimenting with his own free-verse style, he began writing the poems that would appear in the slim first edition of *Leaves of Grass* in 1855. It was at the time of publication that he began calling himself "Walt" instead of "Walter." The inaugural collection, of which fewer than 800 copies were printed, consisted of just 12 poems and was far from a commercial or popular success. It did find favor, however, with such notables as Henry David Thoreau, who called the poet "superhuman," and Ralph Waldo Emerson, who wrote to the author: "I find it the most extraordinary piece of wit and wisdom that America has yet contributed. . . . I greet you at the beginning of a great career."

As later generations of readers and critics would concur, Whitman's verse captured the pulse of a young nation with subject matter as free as the democratic principles he championed, rhythms and forms as unfettered as its masses of humanity, and a brash disregard for cultural norms that was shocking to genteel contemporaries. His attention to everyday experience—labor, sexuality, and the simple joys of living—evoked images that some believed threatened American social values but most others ultimately embraced. Rejecting "poetic diction" in the conventional sense, Whitman introduced a new language to American

Walt Whitman's free-verse collection *Leaves of Grass*, a celebration of everyday experience and "the American masses," earned him a reputation as "poet of democracy."

verse, including slang, colloquialisms, neologisms, and foreign words and phrases. Abandoning the regular meters and stanzaic patterns of traditional English-language poetry, he employed long, rhythmic, free-verse lines and natural "organic" structures.

Whitman continued to revise, extend, and republish *Leaves of Grass* for the rest of his life. The second edition, with 20 additional poems, appeared in 1856, followed by four more editions by 1872. Scholars generally count three more in the succeeding years, including the "deathbed edition" in 1892. In its final form, the collection contained nearly 400 poems.

In both content and technique, each new edition was groundbreaking. Reflecting Whitman's passionate commitment to the democratic ideal, two themes dominated throughout: the freedom and dignity of the individual, and the equality of all people. The poems in each release added depth, dimension, and energy to his portrayal of the American masses, testing social norms and the limits of artistic expression in new ways. Increasingly prominent themes included the beauty and innocence of the human body, with extensive allusions to sexual expression and homoerotic attraction. Modern critics credit Whitman with writing some of the first openly gay material in American literature. The 1881–1882 edition of *Leaves*, the seventh in all, was arguably the most controversial. The volume was banned in Boston because of its many sexual innuendos, but Whitman stood firm in not changing the controversial material.

Wartime Volunteerism and Other Pursuits

Although he despised the righteousness and self-importance of abolitionists, Whitman denounced slavery in an 1856 political tract titled *The Eighteenth Presidency*, a prophecy of the election of Abraham Lincoln in 1860. Whitman tended toward a fierce patriotism and worried that potential assassins in New York City endangered the president-elect, whom the poet regarded as humble but shrewd. During the course of the Civil War, Whitman rallied Northerners to support the Union with the poem "Beat! Beat! Drums!" (1865) and advocated the mustering of black regiments.

Fearing for the survival of his brother George, a lieutenant colonel in the Union army, Whitman traveled south on foot to Virginia after the Battle of Fredericksburg in December 1862. Although he found his brother with only a superficial wound to the cheek, Whitman's visit among the casualties prompted him to move to Washington, D.C., to volunteer as a nurse and stretcher bearer. Like Louisa May Alcott at the same time, Whitman tended to the wounded and sent newspaper dispatches and letters to family back North. In off hours, he wrote and worked part-time in the military paymaster's office. His war poems, collected in *Drum-Taps* (1865, later incorporated in *Leaves of Grass*), included such vivid accounts as "The Wound-Dresser," which describes the bandaging of the wounded and dying.

When the war ended, Whitman remained in Washington to work as a clerk in the U.S. attorney general's office, during which time he became involved in a romantic relationship with a former Confederate soldier that would last a number of years. In April 1865, the martyrdom of President Lincoln occasioned two of Whitman's most popular poems, "O Captain! My Captain!" and "When Lilacs Last in the Dooryard Bloom'd," both tributes to the slain commander in chief that appeared in a 24-page insert titled *Sequel to Drum-Taps* (1865–1866).

The publication in England of the *Poems of Walt Whitman* (1868) finally began spreading the poet's reputation; his fame and critical acclaim continued to grow until the end of his life and beyond. In the meantime, Whitman wrote with ardor and ambivalence about the state of the nation during the Reconstruction era. In the poem "Passage to India" (1870), he celebrates the American workingman and "the great achievements of the present." But in *Democratic Vistas* (1871), perhaps his greatest prose work, he rails against rampant political corruption and rabid acquisitiveness. Regretting the passage of artisanal, agrarian culture and its replacement by large-scale industrialism, Whitman presaged the values of the Gilded Age: "In business (this all-devouring modern word, business), the one sole object is, by any means, pecuniary gain. The magician's serpent in the fable ate up all the other serpents; and money-making is our magician's serpent, remaining to-day sole master of the field."

After suffering a paralytic stroke in early 1873, Whitman left Washington and moved to Camden, New Jersey, under the care of his brother George. In declining health and increasing pain, he occupied himself with writing for newspapers and magazines, issuing new editions of *Leaves of Grass,* and studying photography; final editions of *Leaves* included photographic self-portraits. By his later years, Whitman was famous throughout the world, not least among writers, artists, and homosexual activists. Among the many who visited his Camden home were the English poet and pioneering gay advocate Edward Carpenter and the Irish poet and playwright Oscar Wilde.

In spite of his many doubts and frustrations, Whitman never lost faith in the future possibilities of a truly democratic America. His death from pneumonia and tuberculosis on March 26, 1892, drew hundreds of mourners to his home.

Gavin J. Wilk, Mary Ellen Snodgrass, and Donald D. Kummings

See also: Alcott, Louisa May; Dickinson, Emily; Lincoln, Abraham

◇◇

Selected Poems, 1855–1865

◇◇

The signature poem of his landmark collection Leaves of Grass, *Walt Whitman's "Song of Myself" appeared untitled in the original 1855 collection. An exuberant affirmation of the universal self, the democratic spirit, and the joys of everyday living, the poem comprises more than 1,300 lines in 52 sections; the first stanza is presented below. Likewise epitomizing Whitman's free-verse style and celebration of democratic values, "I Hear America Singing" was added for the 1860 edition of* Leaves *and became one of his best-known poems; it is reproduced here in its entirety. Also among Whitman's most acclaimed poems are two from the Civil War era: "The Wound-Dresser," drawing on his experience as a military nurse tending to battlefield casualties; and "O Captain! My Captain!," a metaphor in traditional verse form about the assassination of President Lincoln and its effect on the nation—with the commander in chief as the Captain and the United States as the ship of state.*

"Song of Myself" (first verse), 1855

I Celebrate myself, and sing myself,
And what I assume you shall assume,
For every atom belonging to me as good belongs to you.
I loafe and invite my soul,
I lean and loafe at my ease observing a spear of summer grass.
My tongue, every atom of my blood, form'd from this soil, this air,
Born here of parents born here from parents the same, and their parents the same,
I, now thirty-seven years old in perfect health begin,
Hoping to cease not till death.
Creeds and schools in abeyance,
Retiring back a while sufficed at what they are, but never forgotten,
I harbour for good or bad, I permit to speak at every hazard,
Nature without check with original energy.

Source: Walt Whitman, *Leaves of Grass* (Brooklyn, NY: Walt Whitman, 1855).

"I Hear America Singing," 1860

I hear America singing, the varied carols I hear,
Those of mechanics, each one singing his as it should be blithe and strong,
The carpenter singing his as he measures his plank or beam,
The mason singing his as he makes ready for work, or leaves off work,
The boatman singing what belongs to him in his boat, the deckhand singing on the steamboat deck,
The shoemaker singing as he sits on his bench, the hatter singing as he stands,
The wood-cutter's song, the ploughboy's on his way in the morning, or at noon intermission or at sundown,
The delicious singing of the mother, or of the young wife at work, or of the girl sewing or washing,
Each singing what belongs to him or her and to none else,
The day what belongs to the day—at night the party of young fellows, robust, friendly,
Singing with open mouths their strong melodious songs.

"The Wound-Dresser," 1863

1

An old man bending I come among new faces,
Years looking backward resuming in answer to children,
Come tell us old man, as from young men and maidens that love me,
(Arous'd and angry, I'd thought to beat the alarum, and urge relentless war,
But soon my fingers fail'd me, my face droop'd and I resign'd myself,
To sit by the wounded and soothe them, or silently watch the dead;)
Years hence of these scenes, of these furious passions, these chances,

Of unsurpass'd heroes, (was one side so brave? the other was equally brave;)
Now be witness again, paint the mightiest armies of earth,
Of those armies so rapid so wondrous what saw you to tell us?
What stays with you latest and deepest? of curious panics,
Of hard-fought engagements or sieges tremendous what deepest remains?

2

O maidens and young men I love and that love me,
What you ask of my days those the strangest and sudden your talking recalls,
Soldier alert I arrive after a long march cover'd with sweat and dust,
In the nick of time I come, plunge in the fight, loudly shout in the rush of successful charge,
Enter the captur'd works—yet lo, like a swift-running river they fade,
Pass and are gone they fade—I dwell not on soldiers' perils or soldiers' joys,
(Both I remember well—many the hardships, few the joys, yet I was content.)
But in silence, in dreams' projections,
While the world of gain and appearance and mirth goes on,
So soon what is over forgotten, and waves wash the imprints off the sand,
With hinged knees returning I enter the doors (while for you up there,
Whoever you are, follow without noise and be of strong heart).

Bearing the bandages, water and sponge,
Straight and swift to my wounded I go,
Where they lie on the ground after the battle brought in,
Where their priceless blood reddens the grass, the ground,
Or to the rows of the hospital tent, or under the roof'd hospital,

To the long rows of cots up and down each side I return,
To each and all one after another I draw near, not one do I miss,
An attendant follows holding a tray, he carries a refuse pail,
Soon to be fill'd with clotted rags and blood, emptied, and fill'd again.

I onward go, I stop,
With hinged knees and steady hand to dress wounds,
I am firm with each, the pangs are sharp yet unavoidable,
One turns to me his appealing eyes—poor boy! I never knew you,
Yet I think I could not refuse this moment to die for you, if that would save you.

3

On, on I go, (open doors of time! open hospital doors!)
The crush'd head I dress, (poor crazed hand tear not the bandage away,)
The neck of the cavalry-man with the bullet through and through examine,
Hard the breathing rattles, quite glazed already the eye, yet life struggles hard,
(Come sweet death! be persuaded O beautiful death!
In mercy come quickly.)

From the stump of the arm, the amputated hand,
I undo the clotted lint, remove the slough, wash off the matter and blood,
Back on his pillow the soldier bends with curv'd neck and side falling head,
His eyes are closed, his face is pale, he dares not look on the bloody stump,
And has not yet look'd on it.
I dress a wound in the side, deep, deep,
But a day or two more, for see the frame all wasted and sinking,

And the yellow-blue countenance see.
I dress the perforated shoulder, the foot with the bullet-wound,
Cleanse the one with a gnawing and putrid gangrene, so sickening, so offensive,
While the attendant stands behind aside me holding the tray and pail.

I am faithful, I do not give out,
The fractur'd thigh, the knee, the wound in the abdomen,
These and more I dress with impassive hand, (yet deep in my breast a fire, a burning flame.)

4

Thus in silence in dreams' projections,
Returning, resuming, I thread my way through the hospitals,
The hurt and wounded I pacify with soothing hand,
I sit by the restless all the dark night, some are so young,
Some suffer so much, I recall the experience sweet and sad,
(Many a soldier's loving arms about this neck have cross'd and rested,
Many a soldier's kiss dwells on these bearded lips.)

"O Captain! My Captain!" 1865

O Captain! my Captain! our fearful trip is done;
The ship has weather'd every rack, the prize we sought is won;
The port is near, the bells I hear, the people all exulting,
While follow eyes the steady keel, the vessel grim and daring:
But O heart! heart! heart!
O the bleeding drops of red,
Where on the deck my Captain lies,
Fallen cold and dead.

O Captain! my Captain! rise up and hear the bells;
Rise up—for you the flag is flung—for you the bugle trills;

For you bouquets and ribbon'd wreaths—for you the shores a-crowding;
For you they call, the swaying mass, their eager faces turning;
Here Captain! dear father!
This arm beneath your head;
It is some dream that on the deck,
You've fallen cold and dead.

My Captain does not answer, his lips are pale and still;
My father does not feel my arm, he has no pulse nor will;
The ship is anchor'd safe and sound, its voyage closed and done;
From fearful trip, the victor ship, comes in with object won;
Exult, O shores, and ring, O bells!
But I, with mournful tread,
Walk the deck my Captain lies,
Fallen cold and dead.

Source: Bartleby.com (www.bartleby.com).

Bibliography

Berlin, Ira, et al., eds. *Free at Last: A Documentary History of Slavery, Freedom, and the Civil War.* New York: New Press, 1992.

Blassingame, John W. *The Slave Community: Plantation Life in the Antebellum South.* Rev. ed. New York: Oxford University Press, 1979.

Blight, David W. *Frederick Douglass' Civil War: Keeping Faith in Jubilee.* Baton Rouge: Louisiana State University Press, 1989.

Bordewich, Fergus M. *Bound for Canaan: The Epic Story of the Underground Railroad, America's First Integrated Civil Rights Movement.* New York: Amistad, 2006.

Boritt, Gabor. *The Gettysburg Gospel: The Lincoln Speech That Nobody Knows.* New York: Simon & Schuster, 2006.

Boyd, Melba J. *Discarded Legacy: Politics and Poetics in the Life of Frances Ellen Watkins Harper.* Detroit: Wayne State University Press, 1994.

Brands, H.W. *The Man Who Saved the Union: Ulysses Grant in War and Peace.* New York: Doubleday, 2012.

Bunting, Josiah, III. *Ulysses S. Grant.* New York: Times Books, 2004.

Cheever, Susan. *Louisa May Alcott.* New York: Simon & Schuster, 2010.

Chesnut, Mary Boykin. *Mary Chesnut's Civil War.* Edited by C. Vann Woodward. New Haven, CT: Yale University Press, 1981.

———. *The Private Mary Chesnut: The Unpublished Civil War Diaries.* New York: Oxford University Press, 1984.

Clark, Beverly Lyon, ed. *Louisa May Alcott: The Contemporary Reviews.* New York: Cambridge University Press, 2004.

Clifford, Deborah Pickman. *Mine Eyes Have Seen the Glory: A Biography of Julia Ward Howe.* Boston: Little, Brown, 1979.

Davis, David Brion. *Inhuman Bondage: The Rise and Fall of Slavery in the New World.* New York: Oxford University Press, 2006.

Dickerson, Donna Lee, ed. *The Reconstruction Era: Primary Documents on Events from 1865 to 1877.* Westport, CT: Greenwood, 2003.

Donald, David Herbert. *Lincoln.* New York: Simon & Schuster, 1995.

Foner, Philip S. *Frederick Douglass: A Biography.* New York: Citadel, 1964.

———. *Reconstruction: America's Unfinished Revolution, 1863–1877.* New York: Perennial Classics, 2002.

Foster, Frances Smith, ed. *A Brighter Coming Day: A Frances Watkins Harper Reader.* New York: Feminist Press, 1990.

Garfield, Deborah M., and Rafia Zafar, eds. *Harriet Jacobs and* Incidents in the Life of a Slave Girl: *New Critical Essays.* New York: Cambridge University Press, 1996.

Garrison, William Lloyd. *William Lloyd Garrison and the Fight Against Slavery: Selections from* The Liberator. Bedford Series in History and Culture. New York: St. Martin's, 1994.

Gates, Henry Louis, Jr., ed. *The Classic Slave Narratives.* New York: New American Library, 1987.

Gifford, Terry, ed. *John Muir: His Life and Letters and Other Writings.* London: Baton Wicks, 1996.

Goodwin, Doris Kearns. *Team of Rivals: The Political Genius of Abraham Lincoln.* New York: Simon & Schuster, 2005.

Hagedorn, Ann. *Beyond the River: The Untold Story of the Heroes of the Underground Railroad.* New York: Simon & Schuster, 2002.

Heidler, David S., and Jeanne T. Heidler, eds. *Encyclopedia of the American Civil War: A Political, Social, and Military History.* New York: W.W. Norton, 2000.

Holzer, Harold. *Abraham Lincoln, the Writer: A Treasury of His Greatest Speeches and Letters.* Honesdale, PA: Boyds Mills, 2000.

Horton, James Oliver, and Lois E. Horton. *Slavery and the Making of America.* New York: Oxford University Press, 2005.

Hedrick, Joan D. *Harriet Beecher Stowe: A Life.* New York: Oxford University Press, 1994.

———. *The Oxford Harriet Beecher Stowe Reader.* New York: Oxford University Press, 1999.

Kaplan, Fred. *Lincoln: The Biography of a Writer.* New York: HarperCollins, 2008.

Keyser, Elizabeth Lennox. *Whispers in the Dark: The Fiction of Louisa May Alcott.* Knoxville: University of Tennessee Press, 1993.

LeMaster, J.R., and Donald D. Kummings, eds. *Walt Whitman: An Encyclopedia.* New York: Garland, 1998.

Loving, Jerome. *Walt Whitman: The Song of Himself.* Berkeley: University of California Press, 1999.

Lowance, Mason, ed. *Against Slavery: An Abolitionist Reader.* New York: Penguin, 2000.

Martin, Wendy. *The Cambridge Introduction to Emily Dickinson.* New York: Cambridge University Press, 2007.

Mayer, Henry. *All on Fire: William Lloyd Garrison and the Abolition of Slavery.* New York: St. Martin's, 1998.

McFeely, William S. *Frederick Douglass.* New York: W.W. Norton, 1991.

McPherson, James M. *Battle Cry of Freedom: The Civil War Era.* New York: Oxford University Press, 1988.

Mitchell, Domhnall. *Emily Dickinson: Monarch of Perception.* Amherst: University of Massachusetts Press, 2000.

Morris, Roy, Jr. *The Better Angel: Walt Whitman in the Civil War.* New York: Oxford University Press, 2000.

Newman, Richard S. *The Transformation of American Abolitionism: Fighting Slavery in the Early Republic.* Chapel Hill: University of North Carolina Press, 2002.

Perry, Mark. *Grant and Twain: The Story of a Friendship That Changed America.* New York: Random House, 2004.

Pollak, Vivian R., ed. *A Historical Guide to Emily Dickinson.* New York: Oxford University Press, 2004.

Reynolds, David S. *Walt Whitman's America: A Cultural Biography.* New York: Alfred A. Knopf, 1995.

Scharnhorst, Gary. *Bret Harte: Opening the American Literary West.* Norman: University of Oklahoma Press, 2000.

Sewall, Richard B. *The Life of Emily Dickinson.* 2 vols. New York, Farrar, Straus and Giroux, 1974.

Snodgrass, Mary Ellen. *Encyclopedia of Southern Literature.* Santa Barbara, CA: ABC-CLIO, 1997.

———. *The Underground Railroad: An Encyclopedia of People, Places, and Operations.* Armonk, NY: M.E. Sharpe, 2008.

Stanley, George E. *The Era of Reconstruction and Expansion, 1865–1900.* Milwaukee, WI: World Almanac Library, 2005.

Stauffer, John. *Giants: The Parallel Lives of Frederick Douglass and Abraham Lincoln.* New York: Twelve, 2008.

Stern, Julia A. *Mary Chesnut's Civil War Epic.* Chicago: University of Chicago Press, 2010.

Stewart, James Brewer. *Holy Warriors: The Abolitionists and American Slavery.* New York: Hill and Wang, 1996.

Turner, Frederick W. *John Muir: Rediscovering America.* Cambridge, MA: Perseus, 2000.

Weinstein, Cindy, ed., *The Cambridge Companion to Harriet Beecher Stowe.* New York: Cambridge University Press, 2004.

White, Ronald C. *Lincoln's Greatest Speech: The Second Inaugural.* New York: Simon & Schuster, 2006.

Wills, Garry. *Lincoln at Gettysburg: The Words That Remade America.* New York: Simon & Schuster, 1992.

Wilson, Douglas S. *Lincoln's Sword: The Presidency and the Power of Words*. New York: Alfred A. Knopf, 2006.
Worster, Donald. *A Passion for Nature: The Life of John Muir.* New York: Oxford University Press, 2008.
Yellin, Jean Fagan. *Harriet Jacobs: A Life.* New York: Basic Civitas, 2004.
Ziegler, Valarie H. *Diva Julia: The Public Romance and Private Agony of Julia Ward Howe.* Harrisburg, PA: Trinity Press International, 2003.

Web Sites

Abraham Lincoln Papers, Library of Congress: http://memory.loc.gov/ammem/alhtml/malhome.html
African-American Odyssey. The Civil War, Library of Congress: http://memory.loc.gov/ammem/aaohtml/exhibit/aopart4.html
America's Reconstruction. People and Politics After the Civil War, Digital History: www.digitalhistory.uh.edu/reconstruction/index.html
Antislavery Literature Project: http://antislavery.eserver.org
Cambridge History of English and American Literature, An Encyclopedia in Eighteen Volumes. Volume XVI: Later National Literature: Part I: www.bartleby.com/226/index.html
Dickinson Electronic Archives: www.emilydickinson.org
Documenting the American South, University of North Carolina at Chapel Hill: http://docsouth.unc.edu
Frederick Douglass Papers, Library of Congress: http://memory.loc.gov/ammem/doughtml/doughome.html
Harriet Beecher Stowe Center: www.harrietbeecherstowecenter.org
"I Will Be Heard": Abolitionism in America, Cornell University Library: http://rmc.library.cornell.edu/abolitionism
National Underground Railroad Freedom Center: www.freedomcenter.org
Nineteenth-Century Documents Project: www.furman.edu/~benson/docs
Poets' Corner: www.theotherpages.org/poems
Ulysses S. Grant Homepage, Keya Morgan Collection: www.empirenet.com/~ulysses
Walt Whitman Archive, University of Nebraska–Lincoln: www.whitmanarchive.org

Index

Page numbers followed by "*i*" indicate illustrations.

For Product Safety Concerns and Information please contact our EU representative GPSR@taylorandfrancis.com
Taylor & Francis Verlag GmbH, Kaufingerstraße 24, 80331 München, Germany

www.ingramcontent.com/pod-product-compliance
Lightning Source LLC
Chambersburg PA
CBHW071359100726
47908CB00004B/1040

* 9 7 8 0 7 6 5 6 8 3 2 4 3 *